THE ULTIMATE GUIDE TO COOKING FISH THE INDIAN WAY

Prasenjeet Kumar

Copyright Prasenjeet Kumar 2015

To economise on costs, this book contains no photographs. However, if you wish to have a look at how the dishes should actually look like, you could either refer to the e-Book version (which you can download for FREE if you purchase this Book under the Kindle Matchbook Programme) or to the Author's website **www.cookinginajiffy.com**.

Cover photo: Fish Chettinad as made in my home.

Disclaimers

Although the Author has made every effort to ensure that the information in this book was correct at the time of publication, the Author does not assume and hereby disclaims any liability to any party for any loss, damage, or disruption caused by errors or omissions, whether such errors or omissions result from negligence, accident, or any other cause.

This book is not intended as a substitute for the medical advice of physicians. The reader should regularly consult a physician in matters relating to his/her health and particularly with respect to any symptoms that may require diagnosis or medical attention.

This book also assumes that the reader does not suffer from any food allergies or related medical conditions. Readers suffering from food allergies are requested to skip the recipes that contains ingredients which trigger adverse reactions in that reader or in his/her family and friends.

The spellings used in this book are British, which may look strange to my American friends, but NOT to those living in Australia, Canada, India, Ireland and, of course, the United Kingdom. This means that color is written as colour and so on. I hope that is NOT too confusing!

Table of Contents

I

Fish—Why Bother?

"When you fish for love, bait with your heart, not your brain".

Mark Twain

"Give a man a fish and you feed him for a day. Teach a man to fish and you feed him for a lifetime".

Chinese Proverb

Nice thoughts above, if you want to use fish as a verb or metaphor. But are you sure you'd like to put that little slimy, smelly thing, that only Penguin and Eskimos appear to be fond of, on your plate?

Do you wonder if there are really some people in the world who instead of plumping for the robust chewiness of the red meat steak prefer instead the "insipid", "characterless" taste of the fish?

Does the word "fishmonger" gives you the same negative ring as do the words "fear monger" or "rumour monger"?

Are you of the firm opinion that a can of tuna is best suited only for your cat?

Then certainly you are not alone.

But you may be in danger of belonging to a near extinct tribe of people who don't realise the enormous benefits of including fish in their diets.

Fish has lately acquired a formidable reputation for being a source of low calorie, high protein, waist-slimming, "brain food," that is bristling with selenium, zinc, iodine, potassium, vitamins A & D and such long strands of polyunsaturated Omega-3 fatty acids that you just can't get from your favourite prime cut of red meat, unfortunately.

Research indicates that even if you're not a fish fan, eating fish only once or twice a week can be enough to reverse the cholesterol laden disadvantages of eating red meat. The National Institute of Health recommends that people consume at least 2 percent of their total daily calories as Omega-3 fatty acids. For an 1800 calorie diet, this comes to about 3.6 grams per day which you can get easily from just two (four-ounce or approx. 100 gram) pieces of salmon.

Yes, you can also get your daily recommended dose of Omega-3 through fish oil supplements; or if you are a strict vegetarian, from such sources as flaxseed,

flaxseed oil, walnuts, canola oil, soybeans and soybean oil. However, similar to the use of non-prescription supplements, the evidence of health benefits from eating these pills isn't as strong as it is from eating fish.

Researchers by now have been able to catalogue as many as ten solid reasons for adding a portion of fish to your diet to improve your overall health:

* Reduce dementia and Alzheimer's Risk: According to a study presented to the Radiological Society of North America, people who ate fish had larger cells in those areas of the brain which are responsible for memory and learning, and which can help lower the risk of cognitive decline leading to dementia or the dreaded Alzheimer's disease.

* Prevent Heart Disease: A Danish study of 49,000 women, that was published in Hypertension: Journal of the American Heart Association, found that women who ate little to no fish had 50 percent more heart problems than those who ate fish at least once a week. Omega-3 fatty acids were otherwise found to decrease triglycerides, lower blood pressure, reduce blood clotting, decrease stroke and heart failure risk, and reduce irregular heartbeats

* Improve Skin and Hair: One of the biggest side effects of following any diet is the adverse effect on your skin and hair. The Omega-3s in fish, however, are the kind of "healthy fat" that can keep your skin

glowing and your hair shiny without adding on to your waistline.

* Ease Depression: Several studies have found that when taken along with antidepressant medicines, the Omega-3s in fish are found to be more effective at treating depression than just prescription medication.

* Boost Brain Development: Omega-3s are also found to boost brain development in children. Some studies have even found Omega-3 consumption to be soothing symptoms of Attention Deficit Hyperactivity Disorder (ADHD) that some children are afflicted with.

* Excellent source of Vitamin D: Fish is a sun-less source of vitamin D, which boosts immunity, improves bone health, and in conjunction with the Omega-3s in fish, wards off cognitive decline. Just one four-ounce (approx. 100 gram) serving of salmon contains 75 percent of your daily recommended amount of this wonderful vitamin.

* Better fertility: While fish is not exactly an aphrodisiac, studies show that men who ate more fresh fish were more virile than those who ate unhealthy diets. Similarly women eating fish during pregnancy appear to have a lesser risk of delivering a premature baby

* Better eyesight: Studies indicate that breastfed babies of mothers who ate fish had better eyesight,

perhaps due to the Omega 3 fatty acids transmitted in breast milk.

* Reduces the risk of developing cancer: Research is close to establishing a link between eating fish and reducing the risk of developing cancers, especially of the oral cavity, oesophagus, colon, breast, ovary and prostate, by 30 to 50 per cent.

* Alleviates inflammatory conditions: - Eating fish appears to also help in reducing the symptoms of rheumatoid arthritis, psoriasis, diabetes, childhood asthma and other autoimmune diseases.

Convinced somewhat? Let's then proceed to how you can include fish in your diet in the most flavourful ways that are known to mankind.

Food for Thought

"Give a man a fish, and you'll feed him for a day. Teach a man to fish, and he'll buy a funny hat. Talk to a hungry man about fish, and you're a consultant."

– Scott Adams

II

Cooking Fish the Indian Way

*"They say fish should swim thrice * * * first it should swim in the sea (do you mind me?) then it should swim in butter, and at last, sirrah, it should swim in good claret".*

Jonathan Swift

"Give a man a fish and he will ask for tartar sauce and French fries! Moreover, some politician who wants his vote will declare all these things to be among his 'basic rights.'"

Thomas Sowell

If you think, like Jonathan Swift above, that fish needs to be cooked only with butter and wine, or like Thomas Sowell that the tastiest way to have fish is with tartar sauce and French fries, then you need to think again.

While there definitely are some fishing communities which love sun-dried, stinky fish, most Asian traditions of cooking fish employ a number of flavourful techniques to mask whatever little "smell" the fish may have acquired in its journey from the sea, river or lake to your plate.

This in the Thai tradition could mean the use of galangal, kafir lime leaves and lemongrass. The Chinese would, of course, be liberal with their soya sauce, chilli sauce and fish oil. The Japanese would often be so frugal with their spicing that they would leave their fish almost raw. But they would compensate that with the most exquisitely carved sushi rolls that your mind can ever conjure.

But the Indians use nothing that the Chinese, Japanese, Thai or the Koreans are so fond of. Instead they seem to dunk their fish in almost everything that grows in their backyards and still manage to come up with a mindboggling number of flavourful preparations.

This book is a humble attempt to catalogue 43 such mouth-watering "Home-Style" ways to cooking fish in a JIFFY as only Indians Can. You will learn to cook with yoghurt and coconut milk, mustard and turmeric, *pachphoran* (mixture of five spices) and *garam masala* (literally hot spices) and so on.

So say bye to the boring boiled and broiled ways to make fish and prawn dishes and let this new book open your eyes to the wonderful possibilities of cooking fish the way Northern, Southern, Eastern and Western Indians do.

There are six starter (or dry) dishes, 14 curries, 12 prawn dishes, and 4 ways to cook fish head and eggs (caviar) the Indian way. For the spice-challenged or nostalgia ridden folks, there are 7 dishes from the days of the British Raj that do use cheese and baking, if you were missing that!

So if you were wondering how to incorporate this superb, dripping with long strands of polyunsaturated essential omega-3 fatty acids (that the human body can't naturally produce), low-calorie, high quality protein rich white meat in your daily diet, just join us on this roller coaster journey of mindboggling seasoning and spices which only the Indians can manage.

N.B. Please remember that the "Home Style" recipes that I have catalogued here are made regularly in my home. You are strongly encouraged to experiment, adapt and add your own variation so that the food tastes like your "Home food".

A word of warning though.

If you are a complete newbie i.e. someone who does not even know how to boil an egg, then I suggest you start from my first book "How To Cook In A Jiffy Even If You Have Never Boiled An Egg Before" (**see the description towards the end of this book**).

Indian cooking can be a little tricky and it is best to acquire some basic cooking skills before making this a part of your daily routine.

Chapter 1

Fish Starters

A wonderful way to introduce fish in your daily diet would be to start with, what else but, the "starters".

We call these "starters" as they serve as excellent cocktail snacks to help start the conversation over drinks; where after they pave the way for the serving of the main course. In this avatar, these are really popular in India during wedding receptions and banquets.

But if you don't have the occasion and the time for "starters", you can always use these ideas as a "dry" dish to be served along any "curry" dish.

You can use whatever fish you get locally and are comfortable with. So for the recipes that we are about to discuss, it doesn't matter whether you get sea fish or fresh water fish. Or whether the fish is de-boned, fillet style or is dressed and cut with bones, steak-style.

For children or those who don't know how to handle a fish with bones, we strongly recommend the use of boneless fish fillets only. Be careful, however, of fish fillets made of smaller fresh water fishes as they may contain some bone fragments unintentionally.

In this background, we now present six starter (or dry) dishes viz. Basic Indian Fish Fry, Spicy Fish Fry, *Tandoori* Fish, Fish *Amritsari*, Fish *Pakoras* and Fish 65.

You can also choose to include Fish Fingers, Fish Cocktail and Fish Chops in this category, which we discuss later in the chapter "The Raj Effect".

Basic Indian Fish Fry

This Eastern Indian Fish Fry recipe is the mildest of all such recipes. You could add yellow mustard seed paste, garlic paste and red chilli powder to spice it up further and turn this into the fiery Bihari *Machheriabhujan.* Roll it up in *besan* (chick pea flour) batter, and fry and you can have the famous Fish *Amritsari* or Fish *Pakoras.*

The variations can be as mindboggling as there are regions in India!

Serves 3-4

Ingredients

Sliced Fish-1/2 Kg (18oz) (2 cups)

Note: If frozen, please thaw the fish first.

Turmeric (*Haldi*)-1 teaspoon

Kashmiri Red Chilli powder-1/2 teaspoon (This imparts more colour and flavour and does not make it hot. Avoid if you can't stand chillies.)

Salt- ½ teaspoon or to taste

Mustard Oil (preferred, otherwise use any other oil that you like) - 3 tablespoon

Method

Sprinkle salt, turmeric and Kashmiri Red Chilli powder on the fish to coat it.

Heat 3 tablespoon of oil in a wok/deep non-stick pan and gently fry the fish @ only 2-3 pieces of fish at a time. After the fish turns a nice golden brown, remove to a plate and add the next batch to the oil.

Please ensure that the fish does not burn.

Your Basic Fish Fry is ready.

Prep time: 3 minutes

Cooking time: 2 minutes @ each batch

Total time: Approximately 10 minutes

Spicy Fish Fry

This is for that lover of Indian cuisine who finds the Basic Indian Fish Fry too mild for her taste.

Serves 3-4

Ingredients

Sliced Fish-1/2 Kg (18oz) (2 cups)

Note: If frozen, please thaw the fish first.

Turmeric (*Haldi*)-1 teaspoon

Kashmiri Red Chilli powder-1/2 teaspoon (This imparts more colour and flavour and does not make it hot. Avoid if you can't stand chillies.)

Ginger paste- 1 teaspoon

Garlic paste- 1 teaspoon

Mustard paste- 1 teaspoon

Lemon juice- 1 tablespoon

Salt- ½ teaspoon or to taste

Mustard Oil (preferred, otherwise use any other oil that you like) - 3 tablespoon

Method

In a bowl, mix together all the ingredients mentioned above, except the oil.

Marinate the fish in this mixture for 15 minutes.

Heat 3 tablespoon of oil in a wok/deep non-stick pan and gently fry the fish @ only 2-3 pieces of fish at a time.

After the fish acquire a nice golden brown colour, remove to a plate and add the next batch to the oil.

Please ensure that the fish does not burn.

Your Spicy Fish Fry is ready.

Prep time: 18 minutes (including marinating time)

Cooking time: 2 minutes @ each batch

Total time: Approximately 25 minutes

***Tandoori* Fish**

This is the dish of choice (from North India) when you want to have your fish with minimum oil and have a barbeque party going as well.

Serves 3-4

Ingredients

Sliced Boneless Fish filet-1/2 Kg (18oz) (2 cups)

Note: If frozen, please thaw the fish first.

Kashmiri Red Chilli powder-1/2 teaspoon (This imparts more colour and flavour and does not make it hot).

Ginger paste- 1 teaspoon

Garlic paste- 1 teaspoon

Garam Masala- ½ teaspoon

Tip: If you can't get ready-made *garam masala* mixture from a nearby Indian store, you can make yours by using 1 black cardamom, 3 green cardamoms, 4 cloves, and 1 inch cinnamon-all ground together for this dish.

Black pepper powder- ¼ teaspoon

Yoghurt- ½ cup

Tomato ketchup- 2 tablespoon

Lemon juice- 1 tablespoon

Salt- ½ teaspoon or to taste

Cooking Oil - 1 teaspoon

Method

In a bowl, mix together all the ingredients mentioned above.

Marinate the fish in this mixture for 1 hour.

Switch on your grill or barbeque.

Remove the fish from the marinade and place it on the grill/barbeque.

Let the fish cook on one side, then flip it gently to cook on the other side.

When the fish acquires a nice pink colour, remove to a plate.

Please ensure that the fish does not burn.

Your *Tandoori* fish is ready.

Prep time: 5 minutes (excluding marinating time)

Cooking time: 15 minutes

Total time: Approximately 20 minutes

Fish *Amritsari*

Named after Amritsar, the famous holy town for Sikhs (and Hindus), this is another classic dish from Punjab, North India that is a favourite party dish as well.

Serves 3-4

Ingredients

Boneless Fish filet-1/2 Kg (18oz) (2 cups); cut into bite-size pieces

Note: If frozen, please thaw the fish first.

Kashmiri Red Chilli powder-1/2 teaspoon (This imparts more colour and flavour and does not make it hot).

Turmeric (*Haldi*)-1 teaspoon

Garlic paste- 1 teaspoon

Carom seeds (*Ajwain*)- ½ teaspoon

Asafoetida (*Hing*)- ½ teaspoon

Coriander seeds (whole)- 1 teaspoon

Chickpea flour (*Besan*)- ½ cup

Rice flour- 1 tablespoon

Baking powder- ½ teaspoon

Dried Mango (*Amchoor*) powder- ½ teaspoon OR Lemon juice- 1 tablespoon

Salt- ½ teaspoon or to taste

Water- 1 cup

Cooking Oil (enough to deep fry)- depends on the size of your wok/deep frying pan

Method

Mix all the ingredients, except the fish and the oil.

Add the water and beat until smooth and light.

The batter should be of a thin coating consistency. Set it aside for at least 15 minutes. This helps the *besan* (chickpea flour) to absorb the water well and attain a thicker consistency.

If it becomes too thick, you may add a little more water and beat well.

Now add the fish to this batter.

Heat oil in a frying pan or wok.

Take the fish in a tablespoonful one piece at a time along with the mixture, and drop into the hot oil.

Be careful of the splatter that follows.

You will find that the mixture swells up.

Gently turn them around and take out from the oil when they are nice and golden brown.

Remove to a dish which is covered with a paper napkin so that all the excess oil can be absorbed.

Repeat till all the fish pieces are fried.

Enjoy with any of the chutneys, specially the mint chutney.

Prep time: 15 minutes

Cooking time: 15 minutes

Total time: Approximately 30 minutes

Fish *Pakoras* (Fritters)

Serves 3-4

Ingredients

Boneless Fish filet-1/2 Kg (18oz) (2 cups); cut into bit-size pieces

Note: If frozen, please thaw the fish first.

Chick pea flour (*Besan*)-1 cup

Rice flour-1/2 cup

Baking powder-1/2 teaspoon

Asafoetida (*Hing*)-1/2 teaspoon

Coriander powder-1 teaspoon

Cumin seeds (*Jeera*)-1/2 teaspoon

Turmeric (*Haldi*)-1/2 teaspoon

Red Chilli powder-1/2 teaspoon

Salt-1/2 teaspoon

Water-1 cup (approximately)

Cooking Oil (enough to deep fry)- depends on the size of your wok/deep frying pan

Method

Mix all the ingredients, except the Fish and oil.

Add the water and beat until smooth and light.

It should be of a thin coating consistency. Set it aside for at least 15 minutes. This helps the flour to absorb the water well and attain a thicker consistency.

If it becomes too thick, you may add a little more water and beat well.

Now add the fish to the batter.

Heat oil in a frying pan or wok.

Take the mixture with the Fish, a tablespoonful at a time, and drop into the hot oil. Be careful of the splatter that follows.

You will find that the fritters swell up.

Gently turn them around and take out from the oil when they are nice and golden brown.

Remove to a dish which is covered with a paper napkin so that all the excess oil can be absorbed.

Repeat till all the fritters/*pakoras* are fried.

Enjoy with any of the chutneys.

Prep time: 15 minutes

Cooking time: 15 minutes

Total time: Approximately 30 minutes

Fish 65

This is the fiery Fish Fry variation from the South Indian state of Andhra Pradesh. Fortunately, this recipe despite the name doesn't need 65 ingredients!

Serves 3-4

Ingredients

Boneless Fish filet-1/2 Kg (18oz) (2 cups); cut into bite-size pieces

Note: If frozen, please thaw the fish first.

For the marinade:

Corn flour- 2 tablespoon

Baking powder-1/2 teaspoon

Coriander powder-1 teaspoon

Cumin seeds (*Jeera*)-1/2 teaspoon

Black pepper (crushed)- ¼ teaspoon

Turmeric (*Haldi*)-1/2 teaspoon

Red Chilli powder-1/2 teaspoon

Ginger paste-1/2 teaspoon

Garlic paste-1/2 teaspoon

Lemon juice- 1 tablespoon

Egg- 1 (lightly beaten)

Salt-1/2 teaspoon or to taste

For the spice mixture

Cooking oil- 1 tablespoon

Chopped garlic- 1 teaspoon

Chopped ginger- 1 teaspoon

Curry leaves- 20 approx.

Green Chillies (deseeded)- 3

Curd- ¼ cup

Black pepper (crushed)- ¼ teaspoon

Red chilli paste- ½ teaspoon

Tomato ketchup- 1 tablespoon

Salt- ¼ teaspoon or to taste

AND

Cooking Oil (enough to deep fry) - depends on the size of your wok/deep frying pan

Method

Mix all the ingredients for the marinade and add the fish pieces.

Set aside for 15 minutes.

Heat oil in a frying pan or wok.

Take the mixture with the fish, a tablespoonful at a time, and drop into the hot oil.

Be careful of the splatter that follows.

Gently turn them around and take out from the oil when they are nice and golden brown.

Repeat till all the fish is fried. Keep aside

Put a pan on your heat source and add one tablespoon of oil. You can use the oil which you have used for frying the fish.

When the oil heats up, add the curry leaves and the green chillies. As soon as these start spluttering, add the chopped garlic and ginger. Sauté for a minute till it starts giving off a nice aroma. Please make sure that your spices don't burn.

Add the remaining ingredients and stir well. Now add the fried fish to this spicy mixture and toss till all the fish is coated well.

Your Fish 65 is ready.

Prep time: 15 minutes (excluding marinating time)

Cooking time: 20 minutes

Total time: Approximately 35 minutes (excluding marinating time)

Chapter 2

Fish Curries

As any observer would readily notice, curries are compulsory in India.

This is so obvious that you just can't miss it. Anywhere you go and you will find curries dominating the Indian meal platter.

Why is it so?

One reason could be the need to have lots of water in a tropical country like India. This need curries could meet in a very healthy (you are boiling your water, aren't you) and appetising manner.

The second reason could be that if you are growing so much rice you would need some curry to "wet" it, to make it less sticky and more palatable. This could be a reason that you have curries in all rice growing regions of the world, be it Thailand, Laos or Myanmar.

Sauces not prepared separately: It is again a very common practice in Western cuisine to boil or bake something first and then to pour on it a tomato or cheese based sauce or flambé it with some wine or such other alcoholic beverage.

In India, only restaurants semi cook their meats and vegetables and prepare some sauces separately; both to be mixed the moment someone asks for a tomato or onion or yoghurt based dish. This is because for restaurants, speed is of utmost essence. So they have to keep ingredients ready in a semi-finished condition for a quick conversion in to whatever dishes the customers demand.

However, "Home Style" (or even *dhaba* or wayside eatery) Indian food is made in one go with everything cooked together. The only thing to "finish" a curry dish could be the sprinkling of some Coriander (Cilantro) leaves.

With this little introduction, let me present to you 14 of the most famous "Home Style" fish curries of India. There are in all 5 North-Indian, 5 East Indian, 1 North-Eastern, 1 Western, and 2 South Indian dishes. Master these and you can rustle up any other fish dish from any part of India.

Masalewali Machhi (Spicy Fish Curry)

This is the common North Indian Fish Curry. Do feel free to play around with the chilli powder quantity to suit your palate.

Serves 3-4

Ingredients

Boneless Fish filet-1/2 Kg (18oz) (2 cups); cut into bite-size pieces

Note: If frozen, please thaw the fish first.

Kashmiri Red Chilli powder-1/2 teaspoon (This imparts more colour and flavour and does not make it hot).

Turmeric (*Haldi*)-1 teaspoon

Onion-3 large (chopped)

Ginger-2 inch piece

Garlic-8 Cloves

Tomatoes-3 (chopped)

(Onion + Ginger + Garlic + Tomatoes blended and made into a fine paste)

Chickpea flour (*Besan*) - ½ cup

Sesame seeds- ½ cup

Black Pepper crushed- ½ teaspoon

Lemon juice- 1 tablespoon

Egg- 1 (beaten)

Salt- 1 teaspoon or to taste

Desi Ghee (clarified butter) - 1 tablespoon

Cardamom pods- 3

Cinnamon- 1 small stick

Yoghurt- ¾ cup

Cooking Oil (enough to deep fry) - depends on the size of your wok/deep frying pan

Method

Put the fish (cleaned and washed) in a bowl and pour the onion, garlic, ginger, tomato paste over it.

Add ½ teaspoon salt, turmeric, lemon juice and red chilli powder.

Marinate for 30 minutes.

Meanwhile combine the chick pea flour with the sesame seeds and the crushed black pepper.

Take out the fish from the marinade but reserve the marinade for the curry.

Dip the fish, one by one, in the beaten egg and roll in the chick pea flour and sesame seed mixture to coat it well.

Heat oil in a frying pan or wok.

Take the fish in a tablespoonful one piece at a time along with the mixture, and drop into the hot oil.

Be careful of the splatter that follows.

Gently turn the fish pieces around and take out from the oil when they are nice and golden brown.

Remove to a dish which is covered with a paper napkin so that all the excess oil can be absorbed.

Repeat till all the fish pieces are fried.

Take another pan/wok and add the clarified butter.

Put the pan/wok on the heat source.

As soon as the butter warms up, add the cardamom and cinnamon.

Wait for a few seconds and add the marinade.

Stir and cook well till it starts giving out a nice aroma.

Add ½ teaspoon salt and the yoghurt and stir well.

Now add the fried fish and let it simmer for two minutes.

Your *Masalewali Machhi* (Spicy Fish Curry) is ready.

Prep time: 15 minutes (excluding marination)

Cooking time: 25 minutes

Total time: Approximately 40 minutes

Fish in Creamy Tomato Curry

Inspired by the famous Butter Chicken or the British Tikka Masala recipe, the bright red curry with its mellow taste will make this dish an instant hit with the young persons in your family.

Serves 3-4

Ingredients

Boneless Fish filet-1/2 Kg (18oz) (2 cups); cut into serving-size pieces

Note: If frozen, please thaw the fish first.

For the marinade

Yoghurt-2 tablespoon

Chopped Ginger-1 inch piece

Chopped Garlic-6 cloves

Coriander powder-1 teaspoon

Red chilli powder-1/4 teaspoon (enough only to add flavour and not to make it spicy)

Cumin powder-1/2 teaspoon

Salt- 1/2 teaspoon or to taste

Cooking oil- 1 tablespoon

For the gravy:

Chopped Tomatoes-3 large ripe

Tomato puree-200 grams (1 cup)

Low fat fresh cream-200 grams (1 cup)

Butter-1 tablespoon

Coriander powder-1 teaspoon

Cumin powder-1/2 teaspoon

Red chilli powder-1/4 teaspoon (enough only to add flavour and not to make it spicy)

Salt- 1 teaspoon or to taste

Sugar-1 teaspoon or to taste

Method

Get the fish ready

The first step to create this delectable dish is to make the fish.

Marinate the fish (cleaned and washed) for about 10 minutes in all the ingredients mentioned for the marinade, except the oil.

In a wok or deep sauce pan, put 1 tablespoon of cooking oil and place it on your heat source.

When the oil heats up, add the fish with the marinade and cook lightly till all the water evaporates.

Don't stir with a spatula as you may break the fish, but you can use it to carefully flip the fish once.

You may instead prefer to just shake the pan gently to ensure that the fish doesn't burn.

Keep aside in a plate.

How to make the gravy

Clean the wok (or take another wok) and put it on your heat source.

Add the butter.

When the butter melts, add the coriander, cumin and the chilli powder.

Let the mixture roast for 1 minute.

Add the tomatoes and cook till the tomatoes soften up.

Add the tomato puree and the salt and sugar.

Gently keep stirring.

As the gravy turns a nice thick red colour, add the fresh low fat cream. Stir well.

Switch off the heat source.

In a microwavable dish, place the fish pieces and pour the gravy over it.

Microwave for 2 minutes so that all the ingredients are well integrated.

Your delicious Fish in a Creamy Tomato Curry is ready.

Prep time: 15 minutes (including marinating time)

Cooking time: 15 minutes

Total time: 30 minutes

Machhi Do Pyaza (Fish with fried onions)

Again a popular North Indian dish that goes well with *Rotis*, the Indian unleavened bread.

Serves 3-4

Ingredients

Sliced Fish --1/2 kg (18oz) (2 cups)

Onion-1 large (chopped)

Ginger-2 inch piece

Garlic-8 Cloves

Tomatoes-3 (chopped)

(Onion + Ginger + Garlic + Tomatoes blended and made into a fine paste)

Onion- 2 large (chopped) separately for frying

Salt--1 teaspoon (or to taste)

Turmeric (*Haldi*)--1 and 1/2 teaspoon (1 teaspoon for marinating the fish and half for the curry).

Red Chilli powder-- 1/4 teaspoon (enough only to add flavour and not to make it spicy)

Fresh green chillies whole--4 (Whole chillies only impart a lovely flavour to the cuisine and will NOT make it spicy)

Mustard oil--3 tablespoon (If you want that classic taste, otherwise whatever oil you normally use)

Water-1/2 cup (roughly 125 ml)

Vessels: One non-stick frying pan and one *kadai* (wok)

Method

Sprinkle 1/2 teaspoon of salt and 1 teaspoon of the turmeric on the fish (cleaned and washed) to coat it on all sides.

Heat 2 tablespoon of oil (the third tablespoon to be used for making the curry) in a non-stick pan and gently fry the fish @ only 2-3 pieces of fish at a time.

After the fish turns a nice golden brown, remove to a plate and add the next batch to the oil.

Please ensure that the fish does not burn.

In a wok, add the oil left from frying (make sure the oil is clean and there are no pieces of fish in it) as well as the fresh third table spoon of oil.

Put the wok on your heat source.

As the oil heats up, add the chopped onions and fry till it turns golden.

Remove from the wok and keep aside.

Now put the onion+ garlic + ginger+ tomato paste in the wok and stir well.

Add the salt, remaining turmeric powder, red chilli powder.

Keep on stirring till the paste is fried and you can see the oil glistening on the sides of the wok.

Add ½ cup of water.

Now add the fried fish to this mixture and also add the whole fresh green chillies and the fried onions.

When the mixture comes to a boil, reduce the heat to the minimum (SIM on a gas stove) and cook it for 2 more minutes.

Your *Machhi Do Pyaza* (Fish with fried onions) is ready.

Prep time: 10 minutes

Cooking time: 10 minutes

Total time: 20 minutes

Thick Fish Curry

Yet another curry dish from North India which very uniquely uses *garam masala* that is generally NOT used in cooking fish.

Serves 3-4

Ingredients

Sliced Fish --1/2 kg (18oz) (2 cups)

Onion-3 large (chopped)

Ginger-2 inch piece

Garlic-8 Cloves

Tomatoes-3 (chopped)

(Onion + Ginger + Garlic + Tomatoes blended and made into a fine paste)

Coriander powder-2 teaspoon

Turmeric-1.5 teaspoon

Garam Masala-1 teaspoon

Tip: If you can't get ready-made *garam masala* mixture from a nearby Indian store, you can make yours by using 1 black cardamom, 3 green cardamoms, 4 cloves, and 1 inch cinnamon-all ground together for this dish.

Red chilli powder-1/4 teaspoon (enough only to add flavour and not to make it spicy)

Cumin seeds-1/2 teaspoon

Cooking Oil-3 tablespoon

Desi Ghee (Clarified butter)-1 tablespoon

Water-2 cups

Egg-1

Sugar-1/2 teaspoon

Salt- 1.5 teaspoon or to taste

Method

Sprinkle 1/2 teaspoon of salt and 1 teaspoon of the turmeric on the fish (cleaned and washed) to coat it on all sides.

Heat 2 tablespoon of oil (the third tablespoon to be used for making the curry) in a non-stick pan and gently fry the fish @ only 2-3 pieces of fish at a time.

After the fish turns a nice golden brown, remove to a plate and add the next batch to the oil.

Please ensure that the fish does not burn.

In a wok, add the oil left from frying (make sure the oil is clean and there are no pieces of fish in it) as well as the fresh third table spoon of oil.

Put the wok on your heat source.

As the oil heats up, add the cumin seeds and let it brown which takes only a few seconds.

Do please make sure that it does not burn.

Immediately add the Onion + Ginger + Garlic + Tomatoes fine paste.

Stir well till the paste starts giving off a nice aroma and you can see the oil ooze out from the sides.

Add the coriander powder, turmeric, *garam masala* and red chilli powder.

Stir well again and add the salt and the sugar.

Now, add the water and the fried fish.

Meanwhile, beat up the egg in a bowl.

As the curry comes to a boil, gently add the egg stirring continuously.

Reduce the heat to the minimum (SIM on a gas stove) and cook it for 2 more minutes.

Your Thick Fish Curry is ready.

Prep time: 10 minutes

Cooking time: 10 minutes

Total time: 20 minutes

Machher Jhol (Fish Cooked in a Light Curry)

A simple fish curry from Eastern India that is eaten almost daily in many homes in West Bengal. This recipe uses a little bit of *garam masala* but no *pachphoran* (mixture of five spices) that most other fish dishes from Bengal use.

Serves 3-4

Ingredients

Sliced Fish --1/2 kg (18oz) (2 cups)

Tomatoes -2 (to be made into a paste)

Onion-1 small (chopped)

Garlic-2 pieces

Ginger-1 inch

(Onion+ Garlic + Ginger to be made into a paste in a blender)

Salt--1 teaspoon (or to taste)

Sugar--1/4 teaspoon

Coriander powder--1 teaspoon

Garam Masala- 1/2 teaspoon

Tip: If you can't get ready-made *garam masala* mixture from a nearby Indian store, you can make yours by using 1 black cardamom, 3 green cardamoms, 4 cloves, and 1 inch cinnamon-all ground together for this dish.

Turmeric (*Haldi*)--1 and 1/2 teaspoon (1 teaspoon for marinating the fish and half for the curry).

Red Chilli powder-- 1/4 teaspoon (enough only to add flavour and not to make it spicy)

Fresh green chillies whole--4 (Whole chillies only impart a lovely flavour to the cuisine and will NOT make it spicy)

Mustard oil--3 tablespoon (If you want that classic taste, otherwise use whatever oil you normally use for frying)

Cumin seeds (*Jeera*)-1 teaspoon

Water-1 cup (roughly 300 ml)

Vessels: One non-stick frying pan and one *kadai* (wok)

Method

Sprinkle 1/2 teaspoon of salt and 1 teaspoon of the turmeric on the fish (cleaned and washed) to coat it on all sides.

Heat 2 tablespoon of oil (the third tablespoon to be used for making the curry) in a non-stick pan and gently fry the fish @ only 2-3 pieces of fish at a time.

After the fish turns a nice golden brown, remove to a plate and add the next batch to the oil.

Please ensure that the fish does not burn.

In a wok, add the oil left from frying (make sure the oil is clean and there are no pieces of fish in it) as well as the fresh third table spoon of oil.

Put the wok on your heat source.

As the oil heats up, add the cumin seeds and let it brown.

Do please make sure that it does not burn.

Add onion+ garlic + ginger paste and stir well.

Add the salt, turmeric powder, coriander powder, red chilli powder, *garam masala* and sugar.

Keep on stirring till the paste is fried and you can see the oil glistening on the sides of the wok.

Add the tomato paste and stir well till the tomato is cooked.

Add 1 cup of water.

Add the fried fish to this mixture and also add the whole fresh green chillies.

When the mixture comes to a boil, reduce the heat to the minimum (SIM on a gas stove) and cook it for 2 more minutes.

Your classic *Machher Jhol* (Fish Cooked in a Light Curry) is ready.

Prep time: 5 minutes

Cooking time: 10 minutes

Total time: 15 minutes

Machher Tak (Fish Cooked In a Tangy Tamarind Sauce)

This is another very popular recipe from the Eastern Indian state of West Bengal using *Pachphoran* (mixture of five spices). Strangely, this dish uses tamarind (and not lemon) to give it an unusually tangy taste.

Serves 3-4

Ingredients

Sliced Fish --1/2 kg (18oz) (2 cups)

Tamarind paste-2 tablespoon

Onion-2 (chopped)

Garlic-6 cloves (chopped)

Mustard paste--2 table spoon (*Kasundi*-ready-made paste is preferred; otherwise just use English mustard paste)

Salt--1 teaspoon (or to taste)

Sugar--1 teaspoon

Fresh green chillies whole--4 (Whole chillies only impart a lovely flavour to the cuisine and will NOT make it spicy)

Red Chilli powder-- 1/4 teaspoon (enough only to add flavour and not to make it spicy)

Turmeric (*Haldi*)--1 teaspoon

Pachphoran: mixture of five spices, that is, *jeera* (cumin seeds), *saunf* (fennel seeds), *methi* seeds (fenugreek seeds), *rai* (black mustard seeds), *kalonji* (onion seeds)--all mixed in equal proportion: 1 teaspoon

Mustard oil (or your preferred cooking oil)--3 tablespoon

Water- 1 cup (roughly 300 ml)

Vessels: One non-stick frying pan and one *kadai* (wok)

Method

Sprinkle 1/2 teaspoon of salt and all the turmeric on the fish (cleaned and washed) to coat it on all sides.

Heat 2 tablespoon of oil (the third tablespoon to be used for making the curry) in a non- stick pan and gently fry the fish @ only 2-3 pieces of fish at a time. After the fish turns a nice golden brown, remove to a plate and add the next batch to the oil.

Please ensure that the fish does not burn.

In a wok, add the oil left from frying (make sure the oil is clean and there are no pieces of fish in it) as well as the fresh third table spoon of oil.

Put the wok on your heat source.

As the oil heats up, add the *Pachphoran* and let it brown (which takes only a few seconds).

Do please make sure that it does not burn.

Add the chopped onion and garlic and stir well till the onions become translucent.

Add the mustard paste and red chilli powder.

Stir again.

Now add the tamarind paste, salt and sugar.

Add a cup of water.

Add the fried fish to this mixture.

Also add the whole fresh green chillies.

When the mixture comes to a boil, reduce the heat to the minimum (SIM on a gas stove) and cook it for 2 more minutes.

That's all. Your *Machher Tak* (Tangy Tamarind Fish) is ready.

Prep time: 5 minutes

Cooking time: 10 minutes

Total time: 15 minutes

Tamater Sarson Machhali (Fish Cooked In a Tangy Tomato and Mustard Sauce)

This is another very popular recipe from the Eastern Indian state of West Bengal using *Pachphoran.* Generous use of yellow mustard gives it a very attractive colour.

Serves 3-4

Ingredients

Sliced Fish --1/2 kg (18oz) (2 cups)

Tomatoes-3 chopped up

Onion-1 (chopped)

Garlic-4 pieces (Tomatoes + Onion+ Garlic made into a paste in a blender)

Mustard paste--4 table spoon (*Kasundi*-ready-made paste is preferred; otherwise just use English mustard paste)

Salt--1 teaspoon (or to taste)

Sugar--1/4 teaspoon

Fresh green chillies whole--4 (Whole chillies only impart a lovely flavour to the cuisine and will NOT make it spicy)

Mustard oil (or your preferred cooking oil)--3 tablespoon

Turmeric (*Haldi*)--1 teaspoon

Pachphoran: mixture of five spices, that is, *jeera* (cumin seeds), *saunf* (fennel seeds), *methi* seeds (fenugreek seeds), *rai* (black mustard seeds), *kalonji* (onion seeds)--all mixed in equal proportion: 1 teaspoon

Water- 1 cup (roughly 300 ml)

Vessels: One non-stick frying pan and one *kadai* (wok)

Method

Sprinkle 1/2 teaspoon of salt and all the turmeric on the fish (cleaned and washed) to coat it on all sides.

Heat 2 tablespoon of oil (the third tablespoon to be used for making the curry) in a non- stick pan and gently fry the fish @ only 2-3 pieces of fish at a time. After the fish turns a nice golden brown, remove to a plate and add the next batch to the oil.

Please ensure that the fish does not burn.

In a wok, add the oil left from frying (make sure the oil is clean and there are no pieces of fish in it) as well as the fresh third table spoon of oil.

Put the wok on your heat source.

As the oil heats up, add the *Pachphoran* and let it brown (which takes only a few seconds).

Do please make sure that it does not burn.

Add the tomatoes + onion+ garlic paste and stir well.

Add the salt and sugar.

Keep on stirring till the paste is fried and you can see the oil glistening on the sides of the wok.

Add the Mustard paste and stir well.

Add a cup of water.

Add the fried fish to this mixture.

Also add the whole fresh green chillies.

When the mixture comes to a boil, reduce the heat to the minimum (SIM on a gas stove) and cook it for 2 more minutes.

That's all. Your *Tamater Sarson Fish* (Fish Cooked in a Tangy Tomato and Mustard Sauce) is ready.

Prep time: 5 minutes

Cooking time: 10 minutes

Total time: 15 minutes

Dahi Sarson Machhali (Fish cooked in a Yoghurt and Mustard paste)

Our tribute to yet another timeless Fish preparation from West Bengal. This dish neither uses *garam masala* nor *pachphoran* and yet is unusually tasty.

Serves 3-4

Ingredients

Sliced Fish --1/2 kg (18oz) (2 cups)

Yoghurt--400 grams (14oz or 1 + 1/2 cups)

Mustard paste--4 table spoon (*Kasundi*-ready-made paste is preferred; or just use English mustard paste)

Milk--1/2 cup

Salt--1 and 1/2 teaspoon (or to taste)

Sugar--1 teaspoon

Fresh green chillies whole--4 (Whole chillies only impart a lovely flavour to the cuisine and will NOT make it spicy)

Mustard oil (or your preferred cooking oil)--3 tablespoon

Turmeric (*Haldi*)--1 teaspoon

Vessels: One non-stick frying pan and one *kadai* (wok)

Method

Sprinkle 1/2 teaspoon of salt and all the turmeric on the fish (cleaned and washed) to coat it on all sides.

Heat 2 tablespoon of oil (the third tablespoon to be used as raw oil later on) in a non-stick pan and gently fry the fish @ only 2-3 pieces of fish at a time.

After the fish turns a nice golden brown, remove to a plate and add the next batch to the oil.

Please ensure that the fish does not burn.

The remaining oil can be strained and kept in the fridge to be used for frying more fish within the next week or so.

It can't be used for anything else because of the fishy smell.

In a wok, beat up the yoghurt, mustard paste, milk, salt and sugar to a smooth blend.

Add the raw mustard oil to this mixture.

Add the fried fish to this mixture and also add the whole fresh green chillies.

When the mixture comes to a boil, reduce the heat to the minimum (sim on a gas stove) and cook it for 2 more minutes.

That's all. *Your Dahi Sarson* Fish (Fish cooked in a Yoghurt and Mustard paste) is ready.

Prep time: 5 minutes

Cooking time: 10 minutes

Total time: 15 minutes

Dahi Macchh (Fish in flavourful yoghurt sauce)

This is another classic recipe from West Bengal. Liberal use of *garam masala*, that is NOT ground, imparts a gourmet twist to this venerated dish.

Serves 3-4

Ingredients

Fish-1/2 Kg (18oz) (2 cups) cut into pieces

Note: If frozen, please thaw the fish first.

Yoghurt--400 grams (14oz or 1 + 1/2 cups)

Milk--1/2 cup

Salt--1 and half teaspoon (or to taste)

Sugar--1 teaspoon

Khada (Whole; NOT powdered) *Garam Masala* consisting of: Green cardamom--2, brown cardamom-1, Bay leaves-2, cinnamon stick-1/2 inch, black pepper-6, cloves-4, and *jeera* (cumin seeds) - 1/2 tea spoon

Onion-1 chopped

Ginger-2 inch finely sliced

Fresh green chillies whole--4 (Whole chillies will only impart a lovely flavour to the cuisine and will NOT make it spicy)

Mustard oil--2 tablespoon (If you want that classic taste, otherwise whatever oil you normally use)

Desi Ghee (Clarified butter)-1 tablespoon

Vessels: Two frying pans and one *kadai* (wok)

Method

Sprinkle 1/2 teaspoon of salt on the (cleaned and washed) fish to coat it on all sides.

Heat 2 tablespoon of oil in a non-stick pan and gently fry the fish @ only 2-3 pieces of fish at a time.

After the fish turns a nice golden brown, remove to a plate and add the next batch to the oil.

Please ensure that the fish does not burn.

The remaining oil can be strained and kept in the fridge to be used for frying more fish within the next week or so. It can't be used for anything else because of the fishy smell.

In a *kadai* (wok), beat up the yoghurt, milk, salt and sugar and make a smooth blend.

In another pan, heat the *desi ghee* (clarified butter) and add the whole *(Khada) garam masala.*

Please ENSURE THAT THE GARAM MASALA DOES NOT BURN.

Add the onion and the ginger and stir well.

When the onions become translucent, add this whole mixture (along with the *desi ghee* in which this all was frying) to the wok containing the yoghurt mixture.

Now add the fried fish, and also add the whole fresh green chillies.

Put the wok on fire, and as the mixture comes to a boil, reduce the flame to a minimum (SIM on gas) and cook for 2 minutes.

Your classic but simple *Dahi Machh* (Fish in flavourful yoghurt sauce) is ready.

Prep Time: 5 minutes

Cooking Time: 15 minutes

Total Time: 20 minutes

Fish *Kofta* Curry

This North-Indian recipe uses balls made of fish mince, which is NOT done in Central Asia from where the original *koftas* are believed to have originated. You can, of course, use any other mince, of mutton, chicken etc, and still come up with a great curry that the young persons in your family will just love.

Serves 3-4

Ingredients for the Koftas (balls)

Sliced Fish-1/2 Kg (18oz) (2 cups)

Note: If frozen, please thaw the fish first.

Ginger paste- 1 teaspoon

Garlic paste- 1 teaspoon

Green Chillies (deseeded and finely chopped) - 2

Black pepper (crushed) - ¼ teaspoon

Garam Masala- ½ teaspoon

Tip: If you can't get ready-made *garam masala* mixture from a nearby Indian store, you can make yours by using 1 black cardamom, 3 green cardamoms, 4 cloves, and 1 inch cinnamon-all ground together for this dish.

Fresh coriander (Cilantro) leaves (finely chopped) - 2 tablespoon

Bread slices- 2

Egg- 1 (lightly beaten)

Salt- ½ teaspoon or to taste

Cooking Oil (enough to deep fry) - depends on the size of your wok/deep frying pan

Ingredients for the Curry

Onion-3 large (chopped)

Ginger-2 inch piece

Garlic-8 Cloves

Tomatoes-3 (chopped)

(Onion + Ginger + Garlic + Tomatoes blended and made into a fine paste)

Coriander powder-2 teaspoon

Turmeric-1 teaspoon

Garam Masala-1 teaspoon

Tip: If you can't get ready-made *garam masala* mixture from a nearby Indian store, you can make yours by using 1 black cardamom, 3 green cardamoms, 4 cloves, and 1 inch cinnamon-all ground together for this dish.

Red chilli powder-1/4 teaspoon (enough only to add flavour and not to make it spicy)

Cumin seeds-1/2 teaspoon

Cooking Oil-1 tablespoon

Desi Ghee (Clarified butter)-1 tablespoon

Water-2 cups

Sugar-1/2 teaspoon

Salt- 1.5 teaspoon or to taste

Method for making koftas (mince balls)

In a deep pan, put the fish and pour water to cover the fish.

Put this on your heat source and bring it to a boil. Boil for 2 minutes.

Meanwhile dip the bread pieces in water and immediately squeeze out all the water. Keep aside.

Switch off the heat source and take out the fish.

If you are using a fish with bones, let the fish become cool enough to touch. Then debone the fish carefully.

Otherwise use a fork to mash up your boneless fish right away.

After mashing up the fish, add all the ingredients mentioned above for the *koftas*, including the bread but except the oil.

Take a tablespoon of this mixture in your hands and shape it like a ball.

Repeat till all the fish is thus shaped.

Now heat oil in a frying pan or wok.

Take 3-4 pieces of the *kofta*, and gently slide into the hot oil.

Gently turn them around and take out from the oil when they are nice and golden brown.

Please ensure that the fish does not burn.

Remove to a plate and add the next batch to the oil.

Repeat till all the fish *koftas* are fried.

Keep aside.

Method for making the Curry

In a wok, put a table spoon of oil and the clarified butter.

Put the wok on your heat source.

As the oil heats up, add the cumin seeds and let it brown which takes only a few seconds.

Do please make sure that the cumin seeds do not burn.

Immediately add the Onion + Ginger + Garlic + Tomatoes fine paste.

Stir well till the paste starts giving off a nice aroma and you can see the oil ooze out from the sides.

Add the coriander powder, turmeric, *garam masala* and red chilli powder.

Stir well again and add the salt and the sugar.

Now, add the water and the fried fish *koftas*.

As the curry comes to a boil, reduce the heat to the minimum (SIM on a gas stove) and cook it for 2 more minutes.

Your Fish *Kofta* Curry is ready.

Prep time: 25 minutes

Cooking time: 20 minutes

Total time: Approximately 45 minutes

Fish Chilly

Obviously inspired by the Chinese, who are just across the border, this dish from the North-Eastern part of India makes a good party dish.

Serves 3-4

Ingredients

Fish-1/2 Kg (18oz) (2 cups) cut into pieces

Note: If frozen, please thaw the fish first.

Onion (sliced)-3

Chopped Garlic- 12 cloves (2 tablespoon)

Green Bell Pepper (sliced) - 2

Dark Soya sauce- 2 tablespoon

White Vinegar- 1 tablespoon

Corn Flour- 2 tablespoon (dissolved in a cup of water)

Salt- 1 teaspoon or to taste

Cooking Oil -2 tablespoon (Use a milder flavoured oil such as groundnut, sesame, or rice bran for the best effect)

Method

Sprinkle a little salt on the fish (washed and cleaned) pieces.

In a wok, add 2 tablespoon full of cooking oil and put it on your heat source.

When the oil heats up, gently fry the fish in batches.

The fish should only have a light golden colour.

Remove the fish to a separate plate.

In the same wok, add the chopped garlic and sauté till it gives a nice aroma.

Immediately add the sliced onions and stir well.

Sauté for a few minutes and add the sliced bell peppers.

Now add the soya sauce and the vinegar. Mix well.

Add the fish and the salt.

Pour the dissolved corn flour over and let this mixture come to a boil.

Reduce heat and cook for 2 minutes.

Switch off the heat source.

Your Fish Chilly is ready.

Prep time: 10 minutes

Cooking time: 10 minutes

Total time: 20 minutes

Meen Moily (Fish Kerala style)

This is our tribute to the robust fish eating tradition of Kerala, the southernmost state of India. This dish bristles with the goodness of coconut milk and coconut powder. The typical "South Indian" taste comes from *Rai* (black mustard seeds) and curry leaves.

Serves 3-4

Ingredients

Fish-1/2 Kg (18oz) (2 cups) cut into pieces

Note: If frozen, please thaw the fish first.

Chopped Onion-1

Chopped Ginger-2 inch

Coconut Milk-200 ml (1 cup approximately)

Coconut powder-2 tablespoon (dissolved in ¼ cup water).

Lemon juice-1

Rai (Black mustard seeds) -1/2 teaspoon

Curry leaves-few

Salt to taste

Cooking Oil -2 tablespoon (Use a milder flavoured oil such as groundnut, sesame, or coconut for the best effect)

Method

Sprinkle a little salt on the fish pieces (cleaned and washed).

In a wok, add 2 tablespoon of cooking oil and gently fry the fish in batches.

The fish should only have a light golden colour.

After removing the fish to a separate plate, add the mustard seeds to the same wok using the same cooking oil, until they crackle.

Immediately add the chopped onion and ginger and stir well.

Sauté for a few minutes and add the curry leaves.

Add the coconut milk and the coconut powder (dissolve the powder in ¼ cup of water beforehand).

Add the fried fish and the salt. Let the mixture come to a boil. Reduce heat and cook for 2 minutes. Switch off the heat source.

Add the lemon juice and your *Meen Moily* (Fish Kerala style) is ready.

This dish goes really well with plain boiled rice.

Prep time: 5 minutes

Cooking time: 10 minutes

Total time: 15 minutes

Parsi Machchi (Fish Parsi Style)

Parsis are the smallest of all minorities in India who mostly inhabit the Western State of Maharashtra. Originally from Persia, and still practising their Zoroastrian faith, Parsis have straddled the Indian industry with such legendary families as that of the Tatas, Wadias etc.

Parsi cuisine is a unique blend of Persian and Marathi cuisine, which is a little less spicy than the Indian and a little spicier than the Persian cuisine.

From their extensive repertoire of non-vegetarian dishes, we present here a classic fish dish.

Serves 3-4

Ingredients

Boneless Fish filet-1/2 Kg (18oz) (2 cups); cut into serving-size pieces

Note: If frozen, please thaw the fish first.

Chopped Onion-1

Chopped Garlic- 6 cloves

Green chilli (deseeded and slit) - 1 (just for flavour)

Lemon juice-1 tablespoon

Black pepper ground- 1 teaspoon

Cumin seeds (dry roasted and crushed) - 1 teaspoon

Fresh coriander (cilantro) leaves (chopped) - 1 tablespoon

Eggs- 2 (beaten)

Sugar- 2 teaspoon

White Vinegar- ½ cup

Salt- 1 teaspoon or to taste

Cooking Oil -2 tablespoon

Method

Sprinkle a little salt on the fish pieces (cleaned and washed) and rub with the lemon juice.

In a pan, add 2 tablespoon cooking oil and put it on your heat source.

When the oil heats up, add the chopped onion, green chilli and garlic and stir well.

Sauté for a few minutes and add the fish in one layer.

Reduce the heat to minimum (SIM on a gas stove).

Sprinkle half the pepper and cook covered for five minutes.

Meanwhile beat the eggs along with vinegar, remaining salt and sugar and keep aside.

Now open and gently turn the fish over and sprinkle rest of the pepper.

Cover and cook again for five minutes at reduced heat.

Remove only the fish pieces from the pan and arrange it on a serving dish.

In the pan now, add the beaten egg mixture and stir continuously at low heat.

Please ensure that the mixture doesn't boil as the sauce will then curdle.

When the sauce thickens, switch off the heat source and spoon the sauce over the fish.

Sprinkle the crushed cumin seeds and garnish with the fresh coriander leaves.

That's all. Your Parsi Fish is ready.

Prep time: 5 minutes

Cooking time: 15 minutes

Total time: 20 minutes

Fish *Chettinad* (Fish cooked in a Rich Coconut Curry)

This is another classic recipe from South India that is served on special occasions in the *Chettinad* region of Tamil Nadu. Liberal use of *garam masala* imparts a gourmet twist to this venerated dish.

Once again, this is a dish that bristles with the goodness of coconut milk and coconut powder. The typical "South Indian" taste comes from *Rai* (black mustard seeds) and curry leaves.

Serves 3-4

Ingredients

Sliced Fish --1/2 kg (18oz) (2 cups)

Note: If frozen, please thaw the fish first.

Tomatoes -2 (to be made into a paste)

Onion-2 small (chopped)

Garlic-4 cloves

Ginger-1 inch

(Onion+ Garlic + Ginger to be made into a paste in a blender)

Coriander powder--1 teaspoon

Garam Masala- 1/2 teaspoon

Tip: If you can't get ready-made *garam masala* mixture from a nearby Indian store, you can make yours by using 1 black cardamom, 3 green cardamoms, 4 cloves, and 1 inch cinnamon-all ground together for this dish.

Turmeric (*Haldi*)-1 and 1/2 teaspoon (1 teaspoon for marinating the fish and half for the curry).

Coconut Milk-200 ml (1 cup approximately)

Desiccated coconut-3 tablespoon

Black Mustard seeds (Rai) -1/2 teaspoon

Curry leaves-few (around 20)

Red Chilli powder-- 1/2 teaspoon

Salt--1 and ½ teaspoon (or to taste)

Cooking Oil -3 tablespoon (Use a milder flavoured oil such as groundnut, sesame, or coconut for the best effect)

Water-1/2 cup (roughly 150 ml)

Vessels: One non-stick frying pan and one *kadai* (wok)

Method

Sprinkle 1/2 teaspoon of salt and 1 teaspoon of the turmeric on the fish (cleaned and washed) to coat it on all sides. Keep aside for five minutes.

While the fish marinates, put a pan on the heat source and DRY ROAST the desiccated coconut and the coriander powder till the coconut turns a nice golden colour.

Switch off the heat source and take out the DRY ROASTED ingredients on to a plate.

Wipe the pan clean.

Now heat 2 tablespoon of oil (the third tablespoon to be used for making the curry) in this pan and gently fry the fish @ only 2-3 pieces of fish at a time.

After the fish turns a nice golden brown, remove to a plate and add the next batch to the oil.

Please ensure that the fish does not burn.

In a wok, add the oil left from frying (make sure the oil is clean and there are no pieces of fish in it) as well as the fresh third table spoon of oil.

Put the wok on your heat source.

As the oil heats up, add the black mustard seeds and let it crackle.

Immediately add the curry leaves.

Do please make sure that the mixture does not burn.

Now add onion+ garlic + ginger paste and stir well.

Keep on stirring till the paste is fried and you can see the oil glistening on the sides of the wok.

Add the salt, turmeric powder, red chilli powder, and *garam masala*. Stir well.

Add the tomato paste and stir well till the tomato is cooked.

Now add the dry roasted ingredients. Stir well again.

Now add the coconut milk and ½ cup of water.

Add the fried fish to this mixture.

When the mixture comes to a boil, reduce the heat to the minimum (SIM on a gas stove) and cook it for 2 more minutes.

Your classic Fish *Chettinad* is ready.

Prep time: 10 minutes

Cooking time: 10 minutes

Total time: 20 minutes

Chapter 3

The Raj Effect

On a whim, the British memsahib decided to enter the smoky kitchen where half a dozen cooks, masalchis (helpers who grind masalas), and sundry assistants were busy preparing the dinner. Everything looked alright, from an Indian perspective, except for the strange piece of cloth that the cook was using to strain the soup. On closer examination, the memsahib found that to be one of the socks of the British sahib!

When the memsahib screeched in astonishment, the cooks patiently explained that they were NOT using one of the clean socks of the sahib!

Imagine the bewilderment of the British who land up in India in the 17th century to discharge their "white man's burden" of civilising the natives. Proud of their clothes, weaponry, language and culture, they first encounter the Maharajas and their fabulous palaces whose wealth and opulence makes the English royalty feel like paupers. And then at royal repasts, they are bombarded with so many strange spices and flavours that go much beyond the simple salt and pepper that were more or less the only "spice" they were accustomed to back home.

But to the credit of the British, they never gave up. They adapted the humble Indian dal (lentil curry) to substitute for their soups. They introduced baking and use of cheese. They got Indians to grow all kinds of European vegetables like cauliflower, cabbage, bell peppers and even potato.

The "fusion" recipes that thus evolved under the British Raj were initially preserved and passed on by the *Khansamas* (cooks) of Clubs, Government Dak Bungalows or State Guest Houses scattered all over India. Now quite a number of restaurants and hotels carry out those traditions with great aplomb.

In that background, we present seven fish gems from the days of the Raj. These are mostly continental recipes but with an Indian twist.

Enjoy!

Fish Fry or Fish Fingers with Crumbs

This is a classic "starter" or appetizer that you will get with your drinks in most clubs in India. Popular with people of all ages, this dish is now quite a fixture in Indian wedding celebrations too.

Serves 3-4

Ingredients

Sliced Boneless Fish filet-1/2 Kg (18oz) (2 cups)

(In case, you need to make Fish Fingers, then cut the fish accordingly.)

Note: If frozen, please thaw the fish first.

Kashmiri Red Chilli powder-1/2 teaspoon (This imparts more colour and flavour and does not make it hot).

Ginger paste- 1 teaspoon

Garlic paste- 1 teaspoon

Lemon juice- 1 tablespoon

Black pepper powder- ¼ teaspoon

Salt- ½ teaspoon or to taste

Cooking Oil - 3 tablespoon

For the coating

Egg-1

Wheat flour- 2 tablespoon

Bread crumbs- ½ cup

Water- 1/4 cup

Method

In a bowl, mix together all the ingredients mentioned above, except the oil.

Marinate the fish in this mixture for 15 minutes.

Now make the coating.

In another bowl, mix together the egg, wheat flour and water well.

In a plate, spread the bread crumb.

Take out one piece of fish at a time, from the marinade, and dip it into the egg-flour mixture.

Take the fish out and gently roll it on the plate with breadcrumbs so that it is evenly coated.

Do this with all the fish pieces.

Now heat 3 tablespoon of oil in a wok/deep non-stick pan and gently fry the fish @ only 2-3 pieces of fish at a time.

After the fish turns a nice golden brown, remove to a plate and add the next batch to the oil.

Please ensure that the fish does not burn.

Your fish fry with crumbs is ready.

If using an Air Fryer

Pre-heat the Air Fryer at 200 degree C (392 degrees F) for 5 minutes.

Follow all the preparatory steps listed above till you come to frying.

At this stage, with a silicon brush, gently brush the bread crumb coated fish pieces with a little oil on both sides.

Place the fish in the Air Fryer in a way that all pieces remain separate and NOT on top of one another.

Air fry for 12 minutes at 200 degree C (392 degrees F).

Repeat till all the fish pieces are air fried.

Prep time: 5 minutes (excluding marinating time) for wok/ pan; Plus 5 minutes if using the Air Fryer

Cooking time: 2 minutes @ each batch for wok/pan; 12 minutes@ each batch for Air Fryer

Total time: Approximately 15 minutes for wok/pan; 36 minutes for Air Fryer

Grilled Fish

This is NOT a cocktail snack, but the main dish for a proper sit-down British dinner. Goes really well with garlic toasts (with or without cheese) and a little steamed corn or peas on the side.

Serves 3-4

Ingredients

Sliced Boneless Fish filet-1/2 Kg (18oz) (2 cups)

Note: If frozen, please thaw the fish first.

Ginger paste- 1 teaspoon

Garlic paste- 1 teaspoon

Lemon juice- 1 tablespoon

Black pepper powder- ¼ teaspoon

Salt- ½ teaspoon or to taste

Cooking Oil or butter - 2 tablespoon

Method

In a bowl, mix together all the ingredients mentioned above, except the oil.

Marinate the fish in this mixture for 15 minutes.

Heat 2 tablespoon of oil in a shallow non-stick pan and gently grill the fish @ only 2-3 pieces of fish at a time.

(You can also use a conventional electric grill if you really like those lovely grill lines.)

After the fish turns a nice golden brown, remove to a plate and add the next batch to the pan.

Please ensure that the fish does not burn.

That's all. Your Grilled Fish is ready.

Prep time: 3 minutes (excluding marinating time)

Cooking time: 2 minutes @ each batch

Total time: Approximately 10 minutes

Fish Cocktail

This is again a "starter" or appetizer that you may get with your drinks in some clubs in India. Tastier and more flavourful than the humble fish finger fry, because it uses *garam masala*, this dish is generally a hit with people of all ages.

Serves 3-4

Ingredients

Sliced Fish-1/2 Kg (18oz) (2 cups)

Note: If frozen, please thaw the fish first.

Ginger paste- 1 teaspoon

Garlic paste- 1 teaspoon

Green Chillies (deseeded and finely chopped)- 2

Black pepper (crushed) - ¼ teaspoon

Garam Masala- ½ teaspoon

Tip: If you can't get ready-made *garam masala* mixture from a nearby Indian store, you can make yours by using 1 black cardamom, 3 green cardamoms, 4 cloves, and 1 inch cinnamon-all ground together for this dish.

Tomato ketchup- 1 tablespoon

Lemon juice- 1 teaspoon

Fresh coriander (Cilantro) leaves (finely chopped) - 2 tablespoon

Bread slices- 2

Egg- 1 (lightly beaten)

Salt- ½ teaspoon or to taste

Cooking Oil (enough to deep fry) - depends on the size of your wok/deep frying pan

Method

In a deep pan, put the fish and pour water to cover the fish.

Put this on your heat source and bring it to a boil. Boil for 2 minutes.

Meanwhile dip the bread pieces in water and immediately squeeze out all the water. Keep aside.

Switch off the heat source and take out the fish.

If you are using a fish with bones, let the fish become cool enough to touch. Then debone the fish carefully.

Otherwise use a fork to mash up your boneless fish right away.

After mashing up the fish, add all the ingredients mentioned above, including the bread but except the oil.

Take a tablespoon of this mixture in your hands and squeeze it into an oblong shape.

Repeat till all the fish is thus shaped.

Heat oil in a frying pan or wok.

Take 3-4 pieces of the cocktail, and gently slide into the hot oil.

Gently turn them around and take out from the oil when they are nice and golden brown.

Remove to a plate (covered with a paper napkin to absorb the excess oil) and add the next batch to the oil.

Repeat till all the fish cocktails are fried.

Please do ensure that the fish does not burn.

That's all. Your Fish Cocktails are ready.

If using an Air Fryer

Pre-heat the Air Fryer at 200 degree C (392 degrees F) for 5 minutes.

Follow all the preparatory steps listed above till you come to frying.

At this stage, with a silicon brush, gently brush the fish cocktail pieces with a little oil on both sides.

Place the fish in the Air Fryer in a way that all pieces remain separate and NOT on top of one another.

Air fry for 10 minutes at 200 degree C (392 degrees F).

Repeat till all the fish pieces are air fried.

Prep time: 15 minutes for wok/ pan; Plus 5 minutes if using the Air Fryer

Cooking time: 2 minutes @ each batch for wok/pan; 10 minutes@ each batch for Air Fryer

Total time: Approximately 25 minutes for wok/pan; 40 minutes for Air Fryer

Fish Chops

This dish also uses *garam masala* but is more suited for dinners than snacks. Most clubs prefer to make this dish with chicken or mutton mince as they are more easily available. That makes this quite a rare gourmet dish.

Serves 3-4

Ingredients

Sliced Fish- 250 grams (9oz) (1 cup)

Note: If frozen, please thaw the fish first.

Onions (chopped) - 2

Ginger (chopped) - 1 teaspoon

Garlic (chopped) - 1 teaspoon

Green Chillies (deseeded and finely chopped) - 2

Black pepper (crushed) - ¼ teaspoon

Cumin seeds (*Jeera*) - ½ teaspoon

Garam Masala- ½ teaspoon

Tip: If you can't get ready-made *garam masala* mixture from a nearby Indian store, you can make yours by using 1 black cardamom, 3 green cardamoms, 4 cloves, and 1 inch cinnamon-all ground together for this dish.

Tomato ketchup- 1 tablespoon

Fresh coriander (Cilantro) leaves (finely chopped) - 2 tablespoon

Raisins- 1 tablespoon

Salt- 1/4 teaspoon or to taste

Cooking oil- 1 tablespoon

For the covering:

Potatoes (boiled and mashed) - 1/2 Kg (18oz) (2 cups)

Salt and pepper to taste

Egg-1

Wheat flour- 2 tablespoon

Bread crumbs- ½ cup

Water- 1/4 cup

AND

Cooking Oil (enough to deep fry) - depends on the size of your wok/deep frying pan

Method

In a deep pan, put the fish and pour water to cover the fish.

Put this on your heat source and bring it to a boil. Boil for 2 minutes.

Switch off the heat source and take out the fish.

If you are using a fish with bones, let the fish become cool enough to touch. Then debone the fish carefully.

Otherwise use a fork to mash up your boneless fish right away. Keep aside.

Place a pan on your heat source and put one tablespoon of cooking oil.

As soon as the oil heats up, add the cumin seeds.

In a few seconds the cumin will splutter and brown. Immediately add the chopped onion, garlic and ginger.

Sauté till it starts changing colour and gives off a nice aroma.

Now add the mashed fish and rest of the ingredients. Mix well and cook for about 2 minutes.

Switch off the heat source.

Meanwhile take the mashed potatoes and add salt and pepper.

Take two tablespoon of this mixture in your hands and make a hole in the middle.

Fill the hole up with the fish mixture and roll into an egg shape.

Make sure that the fish mixture is covered well with the potato on all sides.

Repeat till all the fish is thus shaped.

Now make the coating:

In another bowl, mix together the egg, wheat flour and water well.

In a plate, spread the bread crumb.

Take out one piece of fish chop at a time, and dip it into the egg-flour mixture.

Then take the fish chop out and gently roll it on the plate with breadcrumbs so that it is evenly coated.

Do this with all the fish chops.

Heat oil in a frying pan or wok.

Take 2 fish chops and gently slide into the hot oil.

Gently turn them around and take out from the oil when they are nice and golden brown.

Remove to a plate and add the next batch to the oil.

Repeat till all the fish chops are fried.

Please ensure that the fish does not burn.

Your Fish Chops are ready.

If using an Air Fryer

Pre-heat the Air Fryer at 200 degree C (392 degrees F) for 5 minutes.

Follow all the preparatory steps listed above till you come to frying.

With a silicon brush, gently brush the coated fish chops with a little oil on all sides.

Place the fish chops in the Air Fryer in a way that all pieces remain separate and NOT on top of one another.

Fry for 8 minutes at 200 degree C (392 degrees F).

Repeat till all the fish chops are fried.

Prep time: 20 minutes; Plus 5 minutes if using the Air Fryer

Cooking time: 2 minutes @ each batch for wok/pan; 8 minutes@ each batch for Air Fryer

Total time: Approximately 40 minutes for wok/pan; 65 minutes for Air Fryer

Fish Bell Pepper (Capsicum)

This is a normal lunch/dinner dish. The recipe in a rare flourish uses *garam masala* with capsicum (bell pepper), which the Chinese would never do. But we are talking about the British here, aren't we?

Serves 3-4

Ingredients

Sliced Fish- 250 grams (9oz) (1 cup)

Note: If frozen, please thaw the fish first.

Bell Peppers (Capsicum) - 4 (cut in half with seeds removed)

Onions (chopped) - 2

Ginger (chopped) - 1 teaspoon

Garlic (chopped) - 1 teaspoon

Black pepper (crushed) - ¼ teaspoon

Cumin seeds (*Jeera*) - ½ teaspoon

Garam Masala- ½ teaspoon

Tip: If you can't get ready-made *garam masala* mixture from a nearby Indian store, you can make yours by using 1 black cardamom, 3 green cardamoms, 4 cloves, and 1 inch cinnamon-all ground together for this dish.

Tomato ketchup- 1 tablespoon

Fresh coriander (Cilantro) leaves (finely chopped) - 2 tablespoon

Raisins- 1 tablespoon

Salt- 1/4 teaspoon or to taste

Cooking oil- 1 tablespoon

Method

In a deep pan, put the fish and pour water to cover the fish.

Put this on your heat source and bring it to a boil. Boil for 2 minutes.

Switch off the heat source and take out the fish.

If you are using a fish with bones, let the fish become cool enough to touch. Then debone the fish carefully.

Otherwise use a fork to mash up your boneless fish right away. Keep aside.

Place a pan on your heat source and put one tablespoon of cooking oil.

As soon as the oil heats up, add the cumin seeds.

In a few seconds the cumin will splutter and brown. Immediately add the chopped onion, garlic and ginger.

Sauté till it starts changing colour and gives off a nice aroma.

Now add the mashed fish and rest of the ingredients. Mix well and cook for about 2 minutes.

Switch off the heat source.

Switch on the oven.

While the oven pre-heats, take the bell pepper halves and stuff them with the fish filling.

Place these on a baking tray and bake for 10 minutes at 200 degree C (392 degrees F).

That's all. Your Fish Bell Pepper is ready.

Prep time: 25 minutes

Cooking time: 20 minutes

Total time: Approximately 45 minutes

Fish with Veggies in White Sauce

Again a classic lunch/dinner dish that goes well with rice as well as garlic toast on the side.

Serves 3-4

Ingredients

Sliced Fish-1/2 Kg (18oz) (2 cups)

Note: If frozen, please thaw the fish first.

Cauliflower-100 grams (3.5oz) (half cup)

Broccoli-100 grams (3.5oz) (half cup)

Carrot-100 grams (3.5oz) (half cup)

French beans-100 grams (3.5oz) (half cup)

Peas shelled or snow peas-100 grams (3.5oz) (half cup)

Butter-2 tablespoon (1 tablespoon for sautéing vegetables and the other for making the white sauce)

Salt and Pepper to taste

Wheat flour–2 tablespoon

Milk-500 ml (2 cups; at room temperature)

Cheese Cheddar-50 grams or 2oz (grated) (3 tablespoon)

Method

First sauté the mixed vegetables, which means:

Wash the vegetables thoroughly.

Wherever needed, cut in bite size pieces.

Switch on your heat source and put a pan on it.

Add the butter to the pan and let it melt.

Add all the vegetables and stir well.

Tip: Please don't add salt to the vegetables because the white sauce will contain sufficient amount of salt.

Reduce the heat to minimum (SIM on a gas stove), add the water and cover the pan.

You will see the steam escaping after a while.

Keep checking till the water has dried.

You may also use a fork to poke the vegetables to ensure that they have been cooked properly and are tender.

Keep aside.

Next boil the fish.

In a deep pan, put the fish and pour water to cover the fish.

Put this on your heat source and bring it to a boil. Boil for 2 minutes.

Switch off the heat source and take out the fish.

If you are using a fish with bones, let the fish become cool enough to touch.

Then debone the fish carefully.

Next, Make the White Sauce, which means:

Switch on your heat source and put a pan on it.

Add a tablespoon of butter to the pan and let it melt.

As the butter melts, add the flour.

Gently mix/sauté the flour with the butter making sure that the flour does NOT turn brown.

Switch off the heat source and let the mixture cool down.

When the mixture comes to room temperature, gently add the milk (also at room temperature) and mix well to ensure that no lumps are formed.

Return this to the fire. Add the cheese and a bit of salt.

As soon as the mixture thickens, your white sauce is ready.

Now add the vegetables and the boiled fish to the white sauce and mix well.

That's all. Your Fish and Veggies with White Sauce is ready.

Preparation time: 15 minutes

Cooking time: 10 minutes

Total: 25 minutes

Fish and Rice in Béchamel Sauce

Indians always have fish with rice. But when the British do the same, they do with a twist that is equally delicious.

Interestingly, I could get this "simple" but wholesome dish not only in a few clubs in India but also in the Food court section of the Takashimaya Mall in Singapore's Orchard Road.

Serves 3-4

Ingredients

Cooked rice- 2 cup

Sliced Boneless Fish filet-1/2 Kg (18oz) (2 cups)

Note: If frozen, please thaw the fish first.

Ginger paste- 1 teaspoon

Garlic paste- 1 teaspoon

Lemon juice- 1 tablespoon

Black pepper powder- ¼ teaspoon

Salt- ½ teaspoon or to taste

Cooking Oil or butter - 2 tablespoon

Method

In a bowl, mix together all the ingredients mentioned above, except the oil and the rice.

Marinate the fish in this mixture for 15 minutes.

Heat 2 tablespoon of oil in a shallow non-stick pan and gently grill the fish @ only 2-3 pieces of fish at a time.

After the fish turns a nice golden brown, remove to a plate and add the next batch to the pan.

Please ensure that the fish does not burn.

Keep the Grilled Fish aside.

For the Béchamel Sauce:

Wheat flour–1 tablespoon

Milk-250 ml (1 cup; at room temperature)

Cheese Cheddar-25 grams (1oz) (1 tablespoon)--grated

Butter-1 teaspoon

Egg (beaten)-1

Salt and Pepper to taste

Method

Now, make the béchamlel sauce:

Switch on your heat source and put a pan on it.

Add a tablespoon of butter to the pan and let it melt.

As the butter melts, add the flour.

Gently mix/sauté the flour with the butter making sure that the flour DOES NOT turn brown.

Switch off the heat source and let the mixture cool down.

When the mixture comes to room temperature, gently add the milk (also at room temperature) and mix well to ensure that no lumps are formed.

Return this to the fire.

Add the cheese, the beaten egg and a bit of salt.

As soon as the mixture thickens, your béchamel sauce is ready.

In a baking dish, put the cooked rice and cover with the grilled fish.

Pour the Béchamel sauce over it.

Pre-heat the oven at 180 degrees C (356 degrees F) and bake for about 15 minutes until the dish is golden and bubbling.

Your Fish and Rice with Béchamel sauce is ready.

Prep time: 10 minutes (excluding marinating time)

Cooking time: 25 minutes

Total time: 35 minutes

Chapter 4

Cooking Prawns the Indian way

Indians have a great knack of cooking shrimps, prawns, lobsters and crabs in a way that is unknown to the rest of the world. There is almost nil use of wine, cheese or cream. Unlike the Thai, there is no use of galangal, Kafir lime leaves or lemon grass. There may be some use of the soya sauce in the North-Eastern India but in general mustard will be ubiquitous in the East-Indian preparations, *garam masala* in North Indian and curry leaves, black mustard seeds and coconut milk in South Indian recipes.

While preparing prawns, Indians will de-vein them alright, but generally retain their head and tail as these are believed to enhance the taste of the final dish. These will have to be discarded, with your bare hands, just before you sink your teeth into them, which makes eating prawns a very delicious but messy exercise. Your cutlery will often prove to be quite useless in such a situation!

In that background, we catalogue 12 gems from all the main regions of India. There are 4 recipes from North-India, 3 from East India, 2 from North-East India, 1 from West and 2 from South India.

Enjoy!

Spicy Prawn Fry

This "dry" prawn recipe is quite popular in Bihar, East India, both as an appetizer as well as an accompanying dish to a curry. By playing around with the chilli levels, you can make it as fiery as you would wish this dish to be.

Serves 3-4

Ingredients

De-shelled and de-veined Prawns (of your choice-tiger or shrimps)--500 grams (18oz) (roughly 2 cups)

Note: If frozen, please thaw the prawns first.

Turmeric (*Haldi*)-1 teaspoon

Kashmiri Red Chilli powder-1/2 teaspoon (This imparts more colour and flavour and does not make it hot).

Ginger paste- 1 teaspoon

Garlic paste- 1 teaspoon

Mustard paste- 1 teaspoon

Lemon juice- 1 tablespoon

Salt- ½ teaspoon or to taste

Mustard Oil (preferred, otherwise use any other oil that you like) - 3 tablespoon

Method

In a bowl, mix together all the ingredients mentioned above, except the oil.

Marinate the prawns in this mixture for 15 minutes.

Heat 3 tablespoon of oil in a wok/deep non-stick pan and gently fry the prawns @ only 4-5 pieces at a time.

After the prawns acquire a nice golden red colour, remove to a plate and add the next batch to the oil.

Your Spicy Prawn Fry is ready.

Prep time: 18 minutes (including marinating time)

Cooking time: 2 minutes @ each batch

Total time: Approximately 25 minutes

Prawn 65

This is the fiery Prawn Fry variation from the South Indian State of Andhra Pradesh. Fortunately, this recipe despite the name doesn't need 65 ingredients!

Serves 3-4

Ingredients

De-shelled and de-veined Prawns (of your choice-tiger or shrimps)--500 grams (18oz) (roughly 2 cups)

Note: If frozen, please thaw the prawns first.

For the marinade:

Corn flour- 2 tablespoon

Baking powder-1/2 teaspoon

Coriander powder-1 teaspoon

Cumin seeds (*Jeera*)-1/2 teaspoon

Black pepper (crushed)- ¼ teaspoon

Turmeric (*Haldi*)-1/2 teaspoon

Red Chilli powder-1/2 teaspoon

Ginger paste-1/2 teaspoon

Garlic paste-1/2 teaspoon

Lemon juice- 1 tablespoon

Egg- 1 (lightly beaten)

Salt-1/2 teaspoon or to taste

For the spice mixture

Cooking oil- 1 tablespoon

Chopped garlic- 1 teaspoon

Chopped ginger- 1 teaspoon

Curry leaves- 20 approx.

Green Chillies (deseeded) - 3

Curd- ¼ cup

Black pepper (crushed)- ¼ teaspoon

Red chilli paste- ½ teaspoon

Tomato ketchup- 1 tablespoon

Salt- ¼ teaspoon or to taste

AND

Cooking Oil (enough to deep fry) - depends on the size of your wok/deep frying pan

Method

Mix all the ingredients for the marinade and add the prawns.

Set aside for 15 minutes.

Heat oil in a frying pan or wok.

Take the mixture with the prawns, a tablespoonful at a time, and drop into the hot oil.

Be careful of the splatter that follows.

Gently turn them around and take out from the oil when they are nice and golden red. Repeat till all the prawns are fried. Keep aside.

Put a pan on your heat source and add one tablespoon of oil. You can use the same oil which you have just used for frying the prawns. When the oil heats up, add the curry leaves and the green chillies.

As soon as these start spluttering, add the chopped garlic and ginger. Sauté for a minute till these start giving off a nice aroma.

Please make sure that your spices don't burn. Add the remaining ingredients and stir well. Now add the fried prawns to this spicy mixture and toss till all the prawns are coated well.

That's all. Your Prawn 65 is ready.

Prep time: 15 minutes (excluding marinating time)

Cooking time: 20 minutes

Total time: Approximately 35 minutes (excluding marinating time)

Prawns Tamilian (Prawns cooked in a Rich Coconut Curry)

This is a classic recipe from South India that is served on special occasions in the State of Tamil Nadu. Liberal use of *garam masala* imparts a gourmet twist to this venerated dish.

Once again, this is a dish that bristles with the goodness of coconut milk and coconut powder. The typical "South Indian" taste comes from Rai (black mustard seeds) and curry leaves.

Serves 3-4

Ingredients

Prawns- 500 grams (18oz) (roughly 2 cups)

 Note: If frozen, please thaw the prawns first.

(Only de-shell the top portion and let the head portion remain with the shell. This adds a lot of taste to the curry)

Tomatoes -2 (to be made into a paste)

Onion-2 small (chopped)

Garlic-4 cloves

Ginger-1 inch

(Onion+ Garlic + Ginger to be made into a paste in a blender)

Coriander powder-1 teaspoon

Garam Masala- 1/2 teaspoon

Tip: If you can't get ready-made *garam masala* mixture from a nearby Indian store, you can make yours by using 1 black cardamom, 3 green cardamoms, 4 cloves, and 1 inch cinnamon-all ground together for this dish.

Turmeric (*Haldi*)--1 and 1/2 teaspoon (1 teaspoon for marinating the fish and half for the curry).

Coconut Milk-200 ml (1 cup approximately)

Desiccated coconut-3 tablespoon

Black Mustard seeds (Rai) -1/2 teaspoon

Curry leaves-few (around 20)

Red Chilli powder-- 1/2 teaspoon

Salt--1 teaspoon (or to taste)

Cooking Oil -3 tablespoon (Use a milder flavoured oil such as groundnut, sesame, or coconut for the best effect)

Water-1/2 cup (roughly 150 ml)

Method

Sprinkle 1/2 teaspoon of salt and 1 teaspoon of turmeric on the prawns to coat it on all sides. Marinate for five minutes.

While the prawns marinate, put a pan/wok on the heat source and DRY ROAST the desiccated coconut and the coriander powder till the coconut turns a nice golden colour.

Switch off the heat source and take out the DRY ROASTED ingredients on to a plate.

Wipe the pan/wok clean. Now heat 3 tablespoon of oil in it and gently sauté the prawns till they change colour.

Remove to a plate and keep aside.

Put the wok back on your heat source.

As the oil heats up, add the black mustard seeds and let it crackle.

Immediately add the curry leaves.

Do please make sure that these do not burn.

Now add onion+ garlic + ginger paste and stir well.

Keep on stirring till the paste is fried and you can see the oil glistening on the sides of the wok.

Add the salt, turmeric powder, red chilli powder, and *garam masala*. Stir well.

Add the tomato paste and stir well till the tomato is cooked.

Now add the dry roasted ingredients. Stir well again.

Now add the coconut milk and ½ cup of water.

Add the fried prawns to this mixture.

When the mixture comes to a boil, reduce the heat to the minimum (SIM on a gas stove) and cook it for 2 more minutes.

Your Prawns Tamilian is ready.

Prep time: 10 minutes (including marinating time)

Cooking time: 10 minutes

Total time: 20 minutes

Prawn *Malai* Curry (Prawns in a Mild Coconut and Cream Curry)

This mild but delicious curry is from the Eastern state of West Bengal. Try it once and the younger persons of your family will be hooked on forever.

Serves 3-4

Ingredients

Prawns- 500 grams (18oz) (roughly 2 cups)

Note: If frozen, please thaw the prawns first.

(Only de-shell the top portion and let the head portion remain with the shell. This adds a lot of taste to the curry)

Onion-1 (chopped)

Garlic-4 cloves (large)

Ginger-1 inch

(Onion+ Garlic + Ginger to be made into a paste in a blender)

Garam Masala-1/2 teaspoon

Tip: If you can't get ready-made *garam masala* mixture from a nearby Indian store, you can make yours by using 1 black cardamom, 3 green cardamoms, 4 cloves, and 1 inch cinnamon-all ground together for this dish.

Red Chilli Powder-1/4 teaspoon

Cumin Seeds (*Jeera*)-1 teaspoon

Cooking Oil-1 tablespoon (use a neutral oil and NOT one with strong flavour like mustard)

Desi Ghee (Clarified butter)-1 tablespoon

Coconut milk-200 ml (1 cup)

Low fat cream-200 ml (1 cup)

Green Chillies Whole-2 (for flavour)

Salt- 1 teaspoon or to taste

Method

Place the wok on your heat source.

Add the cooking oil and when it warms up, add the prawns.

Sprinkle a bit of salt and stir the prawns.

Then let the prawns turn into a beautiful pink colour.

Turn the flame to minimum and gently take out the prawns on a plate.

In the same wok, in the remaining oil, add the *desi ghee* and the cumin seeds.

The moment the cumin seeds start browning, add the (Onion + Garlic + Ginger) paste.

Gently stir the mixture and as the mixture starts to brown, add the *garam masala*, red chilli powder and salt (to taste) for the curry.

When the oil separates, add the coconut milk and the low fat cream and mix well.

Add the prawns and the whole green chillies and let the whole mixture come to a boil.

Remove from fire.

That's all. Your *Malai* Prawn Curry is ready.

Prep Time: 5 minutes

Cooking Time: 10 minutes

Total Time: 15 minutes

Jhinga Curry (Prawns Cooked in a Light Curry)

This is how a simple prawn curry is made in most homes in West Bengal. This recipe uses a little bit of *garam masala* but no *pachphoran* (mixture of five spices) that most other fish dishes from Bengal use.

Serves 3-4

Ingredients

Prawns- 500 grams (18oz) (roughly 2 cups)

Note: If frozen, please thaw the prawns first.

(Only de-shell the top portion and let the head portion remain with the shell. This adds a lot of taste to the curry)

Tomatoes -2 (to be made into a paste)

Onion-1 (chopped)

Garlic- 6 cloves

Ginger-1 inch

(Onion+ Garlic + Ginger to be made into a paste in a blender)

Salt--1 teaspoon (or to taste)

Sugar--1/4 teaspoon

Coriander powder--1 teaspoon

Garam Masala- 1/2 teaspoon

Tip: If you can't get ready-made *garam masala* mixture from a nearby Indian store, you can make yours by using 1 black cardamom, 3 green cardamoms, 4 cloves, and 1 inch cinnamon-all ground together for this dish.

Turmeric (*Haldi*)--1 and 1/2 teaspoon (1 teaspoon for marinating the fish and half for the curry).

Red Chilli powder-- 1/4 teaspoon

Fresh green chillies whole--4 (Whole chillies only impart a lovely flavour to the cuisine and will NOT make it spicy)

Mustard oil--3 tablespoon (If you want that classic taste, otherwise whatever oil you normally use)

Cumin seeds (*Jeera*)-1 teaspoon

Water-1 cup (roughly 300 ml)

Method

Sprinkle 1/2 teaspoon of salt and 1 teaspoon of turmeric on the prawns to coat it on all sides.

Heat 2 tablespoon of oil (the third tablespoon to be used for making the curry) in a non-stick pan and gently sauté the prawns till they change colour.

Remove to a plate and keep aside.

In a wok, add the oil left from frying (make sure the oil is clean) as well as the fresh third table spoon of oil. Put the wok on your heat source. As the oil heats up, add the cumin seeds and let it brown.

Do please make sure it does not burn. Add onion+ garlic + ginger paste and stir well. Add the salt, turmeric powder, coriander powder, red chilli powder, *garam masala* and sugar. Keep on stirring till the paste is fried and you can see the oil glistening on the sides of the wok.

Add the tomato paste and stir well till the tomato is cooked.

Add 1 cup of water.

Add the sautéed prawns to this mixture and also add the whole fresh green chillies.

When the mixture comes to a boil, reduce the heat to the minimum (SIM on a gas stove) and cook it for 2 more minutes.

Your classic *Jhinga* (Prawn) Curry is ready.

Prep time: 5 minutes

Cooking time: 10 minutes

Total time: 15 minutes

Prawn Punjabi

Prawns are not native to Punjab but can any one stop the Punjabis to enjoying them in their own earthy ways? Here's then the great *Amritsari* recipe.

Serves 3-4

Ingredients

De-shelled and de-veined Prawns (of your choice- tiger or shrimps)--500 grams (18oz) (roughly 2 cups)

Note: If frozen, please thaw the prawns first.

Kashmiri Red Chilli powder-1/2 teaspoon (This imparts more colour and flavour and does not make it hot).

Turmeric (*Haldi*)-1 teaspoon

Garlic paste- 1 teaspoon

Ajowan (*Ajwain*)- ½ teaspoon

Asafoetida (*Hing*)- ½ teaspoon

Coriander seeds (*Dhania* whole)- 1 teaspoon

Chickpea flour (*Besan*) - ½ cup

Rice flour- 1 tablespoon

Baking powder- ½ teaspoon

Dried Mango (*Amchoor*) powder- ½ teaspoon OR Lemon juice- 1 tablespoon

Salt- ½ teaspoon or to taste

Water- 1 cup

Cooking Oil (enough to deep fry) - depends on the size of your wok/deep frying pan

Method

Mix all the ingredients, except the prawns and the oil. Add the water and beat until smooth and light.

It should be of a thin coating consistency. Set it aside for at least 15 minutes.

This helps the flour to absorb the water well and attain a thicker consistency.

If it becomes too thick, you may add a little more water and beat well.

Now add the prawns to this batter. Heat oil in a frying pan or wok.

Take the prawns in a tablespoonful one piece at a time along with the mixture, and drop into the hot oil.

Be careful of the splatter that follows. You will find that the mixture swells up.

Gently turn them around and take out from the oil when they are nice and golden brown.

Remove to a dish which is covered with a paper napkin so that all the excess oil can be absorbed.

Repeat till all the prawns are fried.

Prep time: 20 minutes

Cooking time: 15 minutes

Total time: Approximately 30 minutes

Jhinga Makhni (Prawns in Rich Tomato Curry)

Inspired by the famous Butter Chicken or the British Tikka Masala recipe, the bright red curry with its mellow taste will make this dish an instant hit with the young persons in your family.

Serves 3-4

Ingredients

De-shelled and de-veined Prawns (of your choice- tiger or shrimps)--500 grams (18oz) (roughly 2 cups)

Note: If frozen, please thaw the prawns first.

For the marinade

Yoghurt-2 tablespoon

Chopped Ginger-1 inch piece

Chopped Garlic-6 cloves

Coriander powder-1 teaspoon

Red chilli powder-1/4 teaspoon (enough only to add flavour and not to make it spicy)

Cumin powder-1/2 teaspoon

Salt- 1/2 teaspoon or to taste

Cooking oil- 1 tablespoon

For the gravy:

Chopped Tomatoes-3 large ripe

Tomato puree-200 grams (1 cup)

Low fat fresh cream-200 grams (1 cup)

Butter-1 tablespoon

Coriander powder-1 teaspoon

Cumin powder-1/2 teaspoon

Red chilli powder-1/4 teaspoon (enough only to add flavour and not to make it spicy)

Salt- 1 teaspoon or to taste

Sugar-1 teaspoon or to taste

Method

Get the prawns ready

The first step to create this delectable dish is to make the prawns.

Marinate the prawns for about 10 minutes in all the ingredients mentioned for the marinade, except the oil.

In a wok or deep sauce pan, put 1 tablespoon of cooking oil and place it on your heat source.

When the oil heats up, add the prawns with the marinade and cook lightly till all the water disappears.

Keep aside in a plate.

How to make the gravy

Clean the wok (or take another wok) and put it on your heat source.

Add the butter. When the butter melts, add the coriander, cumin and the chilli powder.   Let the mixture roast for 1 minute. Add the tomatoes and cook till the tomatoes soften up. Add the tomato puree and the salt and sugar.

Gently keep stirring. As the gravy turns a nice thick red colour, add the fresh low fat cream. Stir well.

Switch off the heat source. In a microwavable dish, place the prawns and pour the gravy over it. Microwave for 2 minutes so that all the ingredients are well integrated.

Your delicious *Jhinga Makhni* or Prawns in a Rich Tomato Curry is ready.

Prep time: 15 minutes (including marinating time)

Cooking time: 15 minutes

Total time: 30 minutes

Prawns in Tomato Sauce

This is a very healthy, low in calories and a quick uncomplicated recipe.

Serves 3-4

Ingredients

De-shelled and de-veined Prawns (of your choice- tiger or shrimps)--500 grams (18oz) (roughly 2 cups)

Note: If frozen, please thaw the prawns first.

Tomato sauce/ketchup-5 tablespoon

Chopped Garlic-1 tablespoon

Butter-1 tablespoon

Salt- ½ teaspoon or to taste

Pepper- to taste

Chopped Fresh Parsley- 1 tablespoon

Method

Switch on your heat source and put a pan on it.

In the pan, put one tablespoon butter.

Once the butter melts, add the prawns and garlic.

Gently sauté till prawns change colour i.e. turn reddish.

Add the tomato sauce, salt and pepper and stir well.

Reduce heat and let the prawns simmer for about 2 minutes. Prawns leave a lot of juice. So there is no need to add any extra water.

Turn off the heat source and take out the prawns with the sauce on to a plate.

That's all. Your prawns are ready.

You can have on the side rice, bread, corn or sauté vegetables.

Prep time: 3 minutes

Cooking time: 7 minutes

Total time: 10 minutes

Stir Fried Prawns with Vegetables

Straight from the North-Eastern states of India, this wholesome dish is full of nutrition. A slight Chinese influence is clearly discernible.

Serves 3-4

Ingredients

De-shelled and de-veined Prawns (of your choice-tiger or shrimps)--500 grams (18oz) (roughly 2 cups)

Note: If frozen, please thaw the prawns first.

Cauliflower-a few florets

Broccoli-1 small

Carrot-1

French beans-a few

Peas shelled-1/4 cup

Snow peas- a few

Soya Sauce-1/2 tablespoon

Tomato Ketchup-5 tablespoon

Red Chilli Sauce-1/4 tablespoon

Salt- 1 teaspoon (or to taste)

Pepper- to taste

Cooking Oil-2 tablespoon (1 tablespoon for sautéing prawns + 1 tablespoon for sautéing vegetables)

Method

Make the prawns:

Marinate the prawns with some salt, half tablespoon soya sauce and ¼ teaspoon red chilli sauce for about 15 minutes.

In a wok/deep pan, add 1 tablespoon cooking oil and as soon as it warms up, add the marinated prawns and sauté till the prawns are cooked.

Remove from the wok and keep the sautéed prawns aside.

Now sauté the vegetables:

Wash the vegetables thoroughly.

Wherever needed, cut in bite size pieces.

Switch on your heat source and put a pan on it.

Add the cooking oil to the same pan and let it warm up.

Add all the vegetables and stir well.

When the vegetables start changing colour, add a pinch of salt and keep stirring.

Reduce the heat to minimum (SIM on a gas stove), add the water and cover the pan.

You will see that steam starts escaping after a while.

Keep checking till the water has dried.

Tip: You may also use a fork to poke the vegetables to ensure that they have been cooked properly.

Now add the prawns and the tomato ketchup and again mix well.

That's all. Your stir fried prawns with vegetables is ready.

Prep time: 10 minutes

Cooking time: 15 minutes

Total time: 25 minutes

You may save time if you buy chopped vegetables from the supermarket. You can also make the prawns and vegetables side by side, if you can spare an additional pan.

Prawn Stir Fried Rice

Another gem from North-Eastern India. Adding rice makes this a complete dish. You may also find this dish on the menu of quite a few "Chinese" eateries in India.

Serves 3-4

Ingredients

Cooked Boiled rice-1 cup

De-shelled Prawns-200 grams (7oz) (1 cup)

Chopped Onion-1

Chopped Red Pepper-1

Chopped Garlic-4 cloves

Tomato Puree-2 tablespoon

Soya Sauce-1 + ½ tablespoon

Vinegar-1/2 teaspoon

Red Chilli sauce-1/2 teaspoon

Sugar-1/2 teaspoon

Salt- ½ teaspoon or to taste

Cooking Oil- 2 tablespoon

Method

Marinate the prawns with some salt, half tablespoon soya sauce and ¼ teaspoon red chilli sauce for about 15 minutes.

In a wok, add 1 tablespoon cooking oil and as soon as it warms up, add the marinated prawns and sauté till the prawns are cooked.

Remove from the wok and keep the sautéed prawns aside. Now, add another tablespoon of cooking oil to the same wok and add the chopped garlic cloves. As soon as the garlic starts giving off a nice aroma, add the chopped onions and sauté till the onion becomes translucent.

Add the chopped red pepper.

Stir well.

Now add rest of the soya sauce, the red chilli sauce, the vinegar and the tomato puree. Also, add ½ teaspoon sugar and salt for the rice. Stir well. Add the boiled rice, and again stir well so that all the ingredients are well mixed. Now add the prawns and again stir well. Switch off the heat source.

That's all. Your prawn fried rice is ready.

Prep time: 10 minutes

Cooking time: 20 minutes

Total time: 30 minutes

Parsi *Jhinga* (Prawns Parsi Style)

Originally from Persia, and still practising their fire-worshipping Zoroastrian faith, Parsis are the smallest of all minorities in India who mostly inhabit the Western State of Maharashtra.

Parsi cuisine is a unique blend of Persian and Marathi cuisine, which is a little less spicy than the Indian but much more spicy than the Persian cuisine.

From their extensive repertoire of non-vegetarian dishes, we present here their classic prawn dish.

Serves 3-4

Ingredients

De-shelled and de-veined Prawns (of your choice-tiger or shrimps)--500 grams (18oz) (roughly 2 cups)

Note: If frozen, please thaw the prawns first.

Chopped Onion-1

Chopped Garlic- 6 cloves

Green chilli (deseeded and slit) - 1 (just for flavour)

Lemon juice-1 tablespoon

Black pepper ground- 1 teaspoon

Cumin (*Jeera*) seeds (dry roasted and crushed) - 1 teaspoon

Fresh coriander (cilantro) leaves (chopped) - 1 tablespoon

Eggs- 2 (beaten)

Sugar- 2 teaspoon

White Vinegar- ½ cup

Salt- 1 teaspoon or to taste

Cooking Oil -2 tablespoon

Method

Sprinkle a little salt on the prawns and rub with the lemon juice.

In a pan, add 2 tablespoon cooking oil and put it on your heat source.

When the oil heats up, add the chopped onion, green chilli and garlic and stir well.

Sauté for a few minutes and add the prawns.

Reduce the heat to minimum (SIM on a gas stove).

Sprinkle half the pepper and cook covered for five minutes.

Meanwhile beat the eggs along with vinegar, remaining salt and sugar and keep aside.

Now open and gently turn the prawns over and sprinkle rest of the pepper.

Cover and cook again for five minutes at reduced heat.

Remove only the prawns from the pan and arrange it on a serving dish.

In the pan now, add the beaten egg mixture and stir continuously at low heat.

Please ensure that the mixture doesn't boil as the sauce will then curdle.

When the sauce thickens, switch off the heat source and spoon the sauce over the prawns.

Sprinkle the crushed cumin seeds and garnish with the fresh coriander leaves.

That's all. Your Parsi *Jhinga* (Prawns Parsi Style) is ready.

Prep time: 5 minutes

Cooking time: 15 minutes

Total time: 20 minutes

Masaledar Jhinga (**Spicy Prawn Curry**)

This is the common North Indian Prawn Curry. Do feel free to play around with the chilli powder quantity to suit your palate.

Serves 3-4

Ingredients

De-shelled and de-veined Prawns (of your choice- tiger or shrimps)--500 grams (18oz) (roughly 2 cups)

Note: If frozen, please thaw the prawns first.

Kashmiri Red Chilli powder-1/2 teaspoon (This imparts more colour and flavour and does not make it hot).

Turmeric (*Haldi*)-1 teaspoon

Onion-3 large (chopped)

Ginger-2 inch piece

Garlic-8 Cloves

Tomatoes-3 (chopped)

(Onion + Ginger + Garlic + Tomatoes blended and made into a fine paste)

Chickpea flour (*Besan*) - ½ cup

Sesame seeds- ½ cup

Black Pepper crushed- ½ teaspoon

Lemon juice- 1 tablespoon

Egg- 1 (beaten)

Salt- 1 teaspoon or to taste

Desi Ghee (clarified butter) - 1 tablespoon

Cardamom pods- 3

Cinnamon- 1 small stick

Yoghurt- ¾ cup

Cooking Oil (enough to deep fry) - depends on the size of your wok/deep frying pan

Method

Put the prawns in a bowl and pour the onion, garlic, ginger, tomato paste over it.

Add ½ teaspoon salt, turmeric, lemon juice and red chilli powder.

Marinate for 15 minutes.

Meanwhile combine the chick pea flour with the sesame seeds and the crushed black pepper.

Take out the prawns from the marinade but reserve the marinade for the curry.

Dip the prawns, one by one, in the beaten egg and roll in the chick pea flour and sesame seed mixture to coat it well.

Heat oil in a frying pan or wok.

Take the prawns in a tablespoonful one piece at a time along with the mixture, and drop into the hot oil.

Be careful of the splatter that follows.

Gently turn the prawn pieces around and take out from the oil when they are nice and golden red.

Remove to a dish which is covered with a paper napkin so that all the excess oil can be absorbed.

Repeat till all the prawns are fried. Take another pan/wok and add the clarified butter. Put the pan/wok on the heat source. As soon as the butter warms up, add the cardamom and cinnamon. Wait for a few seconds and add the marinade.

Stir and cook well till it starts giving out a nice aroma. Add ½ teaspoon salt and the yoghurt and stir well.

Now add the fried prawns and let it simmer for two minutes.

Your Spicy Prawn Curry is ready.

Prep time: 15 minutes (excluding marination)

Cooking time: 25 minutes Total time: Approximately 40 minutes

Chapter 5

Cooking Fish Head and Fish Eggs—the Indian Way

In most world cuisines, fish heads are used to add "drama" to the dish. With eyes intact, they are left to just indicate how big the fish originally was. Generally, fish heads will NOT, in such a case, be touched with your fork.

In Indian, and in basically the frugal East-Indian Bengali cuisine, fish heads called *"muro"* are considered a delicacy. They are cleaned with eyes and gills removed, then chopped in 4-5 big pieces, and then lovingly cooked with veggies or lentils. Of course, no wine, cheese and cream will be used in the process.

Fish eggs as caviar is a prized delicacy in European cuisine with some varieties even claiming price parity with gold. In India, fish eggs are just an accidental by-product of fishing in prohibited seasons (months which don't have an "R" e.g. May to August) when fish generally breed. So fish eggs are a delicacy alright but in an apologetic sort of a way and definitely not in the league of caviar or gold, because that will then endanger fish availability.

With this little pro-environment introduction then allow us to present three popular fish head and one fish egg recipes.

Machher Muro Dal (Fish Head with Split Chick Pea)

This classic Bengali dish comes loaded with the goodness of Chick Pea and coconut powder. Further health benefits are provided by *garam masala*, turmeric, garlic, ginger, cumin seeds and asafoetida.

Serves 3-4

Ingredients

Fish head - 1 cup (cut into half, cleaned with eyes and gills removed)

Chana Dal (split chick pea)-1/2 cup

Water-3 cups (same cup as above!)

Turmeric (*Haldi*) powder-1 tea spoon

Salt—1 and 1/2 tea spoon or to taste

Sugar- ½ tea spoon

Desiccated coconut- 2 tea spoons

Tomato—3 (chopped)

Onion-3 (chopped)

Garlic-2 pieces (chopped)

Ginger-1 inch (chopped)

Cumin seeds (*Jeera*) -- 1/2 tea spoon

Garam Masala (mixture of common Indian spices) crushed -1/2 tea spoon

Tip: If you can't get ready-made *garam masala* mixture from a nearby Indian store, you can make yours by using 1 black cardamom, 3 green cardamoms, 4 cloves, and 1 inch cinnamon-all ground together for this dish.

Asafoetida (*Hing*) - ½ tea spoon

Ghee (clarified butter) - 3 table spoon

Method

Wash the *Chana Dal.*

Put the pressure cooker on your heat source and add 1 tablespoon ghee (Clarified butter).

When the *ghee* heats up, add the cumin seeds for browning.

Add two chopped onions, garlic and ginger.

Sauté for 2 minutes.

Add two tomatoes and sauté for another minute.

Now add the coconut, asafoetida (*Hing*) and stir well.

Add the split chick pea, ½ teaspoon turmeric, 1 teaspoon salt, sugar, water and *garam masala*.

Close the lid and let it come to full pressure (i.e. when the weight lifts and there is a whistling sound).

Reduce heat (to Sim on a gas stove) and let it cook for 10 more minutes.

Turn off the heat source and let the cooker cool down.

Meanwhile sprinkle turmeric and the remaining salt on the fish head. Mix well.

Put two tablespoons of clarified butter in a wok/deep pan and put it on your heat source.

When the ghee becomes hot, add the fish head and fry well. Switch off the heat source. Remove the fish head from the wok/pan and keep aside.

Put the wok/pan back on the heat source along with the left over ghee.

When the *ghee* heats up, add the remaining onions. Sauté well till the onions become translucent.

Now add the remaining tomatoes. Stir till the tomatoes are cooked.

Now add the fried fish head and stir well.

Now open the lid of the pressure cooker and pour the contents of the wok into the pressure cooker.

Simmer for 5 minutes to ensure that everything is well blended.

That's all. Your *Machher Muro Dal* (Fish Head with Split Chick Pea dish) is ready.

Prep time: 15 minutes

Cooking time: 25 minutes

Total time: 40 minutes

Lauki Machher Muro (Fish Head with Bottle Gourd)

This Bengali dish uses *pachphoran*, in place of *garam masala*, but still manages to deliver a tasty punch to the humble bottle gourd.

Serves 3-4

Ingredients

Lauki (Bottle Gourd)--1 (roughly a kg or 2.2 lb. or 4 cups) cut into bite size pieces

Fish head- 1 cup (cut into half, cleaned with eyes and gills removed)

Onion —3 (chopped)

Tomato- 2 (chopped)

Pachphoran, which is a mixture of *Jeera* (cumin), *Saunf* (fennel seeds), *Methi* seeds (fenugreek seeds), Rai (black mustard seeds), and *Kalonji* (onion seeds) in equal proportion--1 teaspoon

Dry Red Whole (not powder) Chilli--1 (Just for flavour and not to make the food spicy)

Turmeric (*Haldi*) - ½ teaspoon

Salt—1 and 1/2 teaspoon (or to taste)

Cooking oil--3 tablespoon

Method Using a Pressure Cooker

In a pressure cooker, add 1 tablespoon cooking oil and when it warms up, add the *pachphoran* and the dry red whole chilli.

As soon as the *pachphoran* starts browning, add 1 chopped onion and sauté it till it becomes translucent.

Add the *lauki* (bottle gourd) pieces, and 1 teaspoon salt. Stir well.

Close the pressure cooker's lid with weight and let it come to full pressure.

Meanwhile sprinkle turmeric and the remaining salt on the fish head. Mix well.

Put two tablespoons of oil in a wok/deep pan and put it on your heat source.

When the oil becomes hot, add the fish head and fry well. Switch off the heat source. Remove the fish head from the wok/pan and keep aside.

As soon as the pressure cooker comes to full pressure, remove from your heat source, cool it under running cold water and release the pressure.

Put the wok/pan back on the heat source along with the left over oil.

When the oil heats up, add the remaining onions. Sauté well till the onions become translucent.

Now add the tomatoes. Stir till the tomatoes are cooked.

Now add the fried fish head and stir well.

Now open the lid of the pressure cooker and pour the contents into the wok.

Stir well and let the bottle gourd (*lauki*) dry up somewhat before you serve.

That's all. Your *Lauki Machher Muro* (Fish Head with Bottle Gourd) is ready.

Method Using Wok/Pan

In a wok/deep pan, add 1 tablespoon cooking oil and when it warms up, add the *pachphoran* and the dry red whole chilli.

As soon as the *pachphoran* starts browning, add 1 chopped onion and sauté it till it becomes translucent.

Add the *lauki* (gourd) pieces, and 1 teaspoon salt. Stir well.

Cover the wok/pan with a lid and reduce the heat to minimum (SIM on gas).

Since gourd leaves a lot of water, you don't need to add any additional water like you do with other vegetables.

Let the gourd cook to your liking for about 10 minutes. It is advised that you poke it once in a while with a fork to see whether the gourd has been cooked well. Meanwhile sprinkle turmeric and the remaining salt on the fish head. Mix well. Put two tablespoons of oil in a separate wok/deep pan and put it on your heat source.

When the oil becomes hot, add the fish head and fry well. Switch off the heat source. Remove the fish head from the wok/pan and keep aside.

Put the wok/pan back on the heat source along with the left over oil. When the oil heats up, add the remaining onions. Sauté well till the onions become translucent. Now add the tomatoes. Stir till the tomatoes are cooked. Now add the fried fish head and stir well. Now add the cooked gourd from the other wok/pan.

Stir well and let the bottle gourd (*lauki*) dry up somewhat before you serve.

That's all. Your *Lauki Machher Muro* (Fish Head with Bottle Gourd) is ready.

Prep time: 10 minutes

Cooking time (with pressure cooker): 10 minutes; with wok/pan: 20 minutes

Total time (with pressure cooker): 20 minutes; with wok/pan: 30 minutes

---

Palak Baingan Machher Muro (Spinach-Aubergine with Fish Head)

This dish, again from Bengal, uses *pachphoran*, in place of *garam masala*, but still manages to lift to the sublime the humble spinach and Aubergine.

Serves 3-4

Ingredients

Spinach (*Palak*)--1 Kg (or 2.2 lb. or 4 cups) (washed and chopped)

Aubergines (Baingan)-1 cup (roughly 250 grams) (washed and cut into 1" cubes)

Fish head- 1 cup (cut into half, cleaned with eyes and gills removed)

Onion —3 (chopped)

Tomatoes--4 (washed and chopped)

Pachphoran, which is a mixture of *Jeera* (cumin), *Saunf* (fennel seeds), *Methi* seeds (fenugreek seeds), *Rai* (black mustard seeds), and *Kalonji* (onion seeds) in equal proportion--1 teaspoon

Dry Red Whole (not powder) Chilli--1 (Just for flavour and not to make the food spicy)

Turmeric (*Haldi*) - ½ teaspoon

Salt—1 and 1/2 teaspoon (or to taste)

Cooking oil--3 tablespoon

Method Using a Pressure Cooker

Heat 1 tablespoon oil in a pressure cooker and add the *Pachphoran*.

As the *Pachphoran* begins to splutter (which takes a few seconds), add 1 chopped onions and sauté on low flame for a minute.

Add the washed and chopped spinach, aubergine and two tomatoes.

Stir the same to evenly mix it. Add 1 teaspoon salt.

Close the lid of the cooker with the weight and let it come to full pressure.

Meanwhile sprinkle turmeric and the remaining salt on the fish head. Mix well.

Put two tablespoons of oil in a wok/deep pan and put it on your heat source.

When the oil becomes hot, add the fish head and fry well. Switch off the heat source. Remove the fish head from the wok/pan and keep aside.

As soon as the pressure cooker comes to full pressure, remove from your heat source, cool it under running cold water and release the pressure.

Put the wok/pan back on the heat source along with the left over oil.

When the oil heats up, add the remaining onions. Sauté well till the onions become translucent.

Now add the tomatoes. Stir till the tomatoes are cooked.

Now add the fried fish head and stir well.

Now open the lid of the pressure cooker and pour the contents into the wok.

Stir well and let the spinach-aubergine dry up somewhat before you serve.

That's all. Your *Saag-Baingan Machher Muro* (Spinach-Aubergine with Fish Head) is ready.

Method Using Wok/Pan

In a wok/deep pan, add 1 tablespoon cooking oil and when it warms up, add the *pachphoran* and the dry red whole chilli.

As the *Pachphoran* begins to splutter (which takes a few seconds), add 1 chopped onion and sauté on low flame for a minute.

Add the washed and chopped spinach, aubergine and two tomatoes.

Stir the same to evenly mix it. Add 1 teaspoon salt.

Cover the wok/pan with a lid and reduce the heat to minimum (SIM on gas).

Since spinach leaves a lot of water, you don't need to add any additional water like you do with other vegetables.

Let the spinach-aubergines cook to your liking for about 10 minutes.

Meanwhile sprinkle turmeric and the remaining salt on the fish head. Mix well.

Put two tablespoons of oil in a separate wok/deep pan and put it on your heat source.

When the oil becomes hot, add the fish head and fry well. Switch off the heat source. Remove the fish head from the wok/pan and keep aside.

Put the wok/pan back on the heat source along with the left over oil.

When the oil heats up, add the remaining onions. Sauté well till the onions become translucent. Now add the tomatoes.

Stir till the tomatoes are cooked. Now add the fried fish head and stir well.

Now add the cooked spinach-aubergines from the other wok/pan. Stir well and let the mixture dry up somewhat before you serve.

That's all. Your Saag-Baingan Machher Muro (Spinach-Aubergine with Fish Head) is ready.

Prep time: 10 minutes

Cooking time (with pressure cooker): 10 minutes; with wok/pan: 20 minutes

Total time (with pressure cooker): 20 minutes; with wok/pan: 30 minutes

Fish Egg *Pakoras* (Fritters)

This is how the Bengalis deal with fish eggs, when they come across these at their fish monger's place. Please don't try this recipe for your expensive caviar however!

Serves 3-4

Ingredients

Fish Eggs- 1 cup (250 grams)

Chick pea flour-1 cup

Baking powder-1/2 teaspoon

Asafoetida (*Hing*)-1/2 teaspoon

Coriander powder-1 teaspoon

Cumin seeds (*Jeera*)-1/2 teaspoon

Turmeric (*Haldi*)-1/2 teaspoon

Red Chilli powder-1/2 teaspoon (just for colour and taste)

Salt-1/2 teaspoon

Water-1/2 cup (approximately)

Onions- 3 (chopped)

Green Chilli- 2 chopped

Fresh coriander (cilantro) leaves- 2 tablespoon (chopped)

Oil for deep frying

Method

Mix all the ingredients except the oil well. Add the water and beat until smooth and light. Set it aside for at least 15 minutes. This helps the flour to absorb the water well and attain a thicker consistency. If it becomes too thick, you may add a little more water and beat well. Heat oil in a frying pan or wok. Take the mixture, a tablespoonful at a time and drop into the hot oil.

Be careful of the splatter that follows. You will find that the fritters swell up.

Gently turn them around and take out from the oil when they are nice and golden brown.

Remove to a dish which is covered with a paper napkin so that all the excess oil can be absorbed.

Repeat till all the fritters/*pakoras* are fried.

Enjoy with any of the chutneys, specially the mint chutney.

Prep time: 20 minutes

Cooking time: 10 minutes

Total time: 30 minutes

On the Side

As mentioned, Indians everywhere like to enjoy their fish curries with simple boiled rice. Occasionally, with dry dishes, or with thicker curries, they may (especially in Punjab) try out *rotis* (the Indian unleavened bread).

No harm then, if I share the recipes for making simple rice and roti too in this book to turn this into a complete Fish Cookbook.

Rice Boiled

Ingredients

Rice-1 cup

Water-2 cups

Tip: Use the same cup please! Otherwise, your rice will NOT turn out to be fluffy.

Wash the rice well (in a vessel 3-4 times, but don't rub it lest the grains break) and let it naturally "dry", on an inclined plate, for 15-20 minutes. This helps enhance the aroma.

If you have a Rice Cooker, follow its instructions. Otherwise, I present three popular methods below to turn out a perfect plate of boiled rice.

Method using a pressure cooker

In a pressure cooker (3-5 litre capacity or 6-11 US pints capacity) bring the water to a boil.

Add the rice to the boiling water.

Close the lid of the pressure cooker BUT remove the weight.

When steam starts escaping from the vent (don't worry, you will hear that typical sound), reduce the heat to minimum. In other words, if cooking on gas, turn the knob to SIM (mer).

Wait for 10 minutes and switch off the gas. Take out the rice. Your hot fluffy rice is ready.

Method using a thick bottomed vessel/deep pan

In a vessel or a pan, bring the water to a boil.

Add the rice to the boiling water. Turn the heat to low and cover the vessel/deep pan with a well-fitting lid.

Cook for 15-20 minutes without stirring the rice. Switch off the heat source. Lift the lid and check whether the rice is properly cooked.

Cooked rice is always soft. To check, you have to take out a grain of rice and press it between your fingers (obviously use a spoon to take out the grain to avoid scalding your hands).

If the grain is still hard, that means it is under cooked. If it is soft, then it is cooked properly.

In case the grain is not properly cooked, you may like to add another ½ cup of water and let it cook on low heat for another 7-10 minutes.

Traditional method (the way it is cooked in villages or dhabas even today)

In a vessel or a pan, bring three (instead of two mentioned in the above two methods) cups of water (for one cup of rice) to a boil.

Add the rice to the boiling water. Turn the heat to medium and don't cover the vessel/deep pan, because the water will boil and spill over.

Cook for 15-20 minutes stirring the rice gently from time to time. Keep on checking whether the rice is properly cooked.

Once the rice is done, switch off the heat source. Drain all the excess water. (You can use a colander. Traditionally, the vessel will just be covered with a lid and the water poured out. This is tricky as both the vessel and the water would be very hot.)

Although the traditional method takes more time, it is believed to bring out the flavours better. Since the water used for boiling the rice is totally drained out, some dieticians claim that this method helps take out some of the starch from the rice thus shaving off some calories from this dish.

Tip: The drained out water can act as an excellent stock for soups especially when it comes out of the local red coloured rice.

Method using a rice cooker

Place the rice and water in the rice cooker.

Close the lid and switch on the cooker. The rice will be cooked and the rice cooker will switch off on its own.

This is the easiest and the most fool proof way of making rice.

Prep time: 20 minutes

Cooking time: 10 minutes with a pressure cooker; 15-20 minutes with a deep pan; and as indicated in the rice cooker manual

Total time: 30 minutes with a pressure cooker; 35-40 minutes with a deep pan

(Excerpted from my book: The Ultimate Guide to Cooking Rice the Indian Way, which contains 34 more such rice dishes.)

The Classic Indian *Roti/Phulka/Chapati*

This simple Indian bread, free of yeast or any other leavening agent, is what many Indian homes have every day for lunch or dinner. It is surprising then that most restaurants don't have *chapatis* on their menus. Instead they focus on making Tandoori *Rotis* or Nans, which they probably find easier to handle when larger numbers are to be served.

For most households, however, it won't be easy to invest in a Tandoor (earthen oven). For them then it will have to be the simple, non-fussy *Chapati*. And here's how you can go about making these.

Note: I have seen people rolling dough with a steel tumbler on any flat surface, or using just their hands to give dough the roundish shape of a roti. I think it is prudent, however, for all newbies to invest in a rolling pin (*belan*) and rolling board (*chakla*) before attempting to make *chapatis*.

Ingredients

Whole Wheat Flour-3 cups (enough for 5 *chapatis*)

Luke Warm Water-1 cup

Method

In a mixing bowl, put 2 + ½ cups of flour, reserving ½ cup as *parthan* (dusting) for rolling out the *chapatis* later.

Add the water and make into a nice firm dough.

Shape the dough into balls about the size of a large walnut.

In another plate, put the remaining wheat flour (the reserved ½ cup), and press the ball into this dry flour.

At this point, take a thick griddle and put it on your heat source.

While the griddle heats up, take out your rolling board (*Chakla*).

Using a rolling pin (*Belan*), shape the dough ball (that is already rolled into the dry flour), into a small circular shape as thin as you can make it.

Now, on the heated griddle place this rolled out *chapati*.

Let it cook a little on one side and then flip over for the other side to also cook.

Using a tong, remove the *chapati* from the griddle and place it directly on the flame.

The *chapati* will immediately swell up and will be ready to be served.

In case you don't have a heat source with a flame, then you will have to puff up the *chapati* on the griddle itself. For this you will need a handkerchief with which you should gently press the edges of the *chapati* as it swells on the griddle flipping it for a second time.

Prep time: 5 minutes

Cooking time: 5 minutes for 5 *chapatis* @1 minute per chapati

Total time: 10 minutes

(Excerpted from my book: Home Style Indian Cooking In A Jiffy, which contains over 100 exotic Indian recipes including for *Poori* and *Paratha*, the two most popular Indian unleavened bread dishes.)

Appendix

An Introduction to Some Basic Indian Spices

It is easy to be overwhelmed with the sheer number and variety of fresh herbs and spices that are commonly used in Indian cuisine. I shouldn't, therefore, make this topic even more complicated by giving the scientific or botanical names of such spices, or where they grow, or how these are harvested and processed. There are many excellent books who have done better justice to this topic.

What I shall attempt here is to just list out some twenty of these spices that you should experiment with when you are just starting out with "Home Style" Indian cooking.

The discerning reader may notice the omission of *Kastoori Methi* (a very fragrant variety of Fenugreek) which is very popular for making curries in Indian restaurants. That's precisely the reason why I am leaving this out from my list. But if you prefer your food to taste like *dhaba* food, do go ahead and stock on *Kastoori Methi* too. Just remember that this is such a strong herb that it will drown the fragrance of all other spices, howsoever expensive they may be. So for heavens, don't use your saffron with *Kastoori Methi* ever!

I am also leaving out some expensive spices like nutmeg or star aniseed as they are hardly ever used in your day-to-day cooking.

Here is then my list, in alphabetical order.

Ajwain

Ajwain or *Ajowan* is pale brown in colour and looks somewhat like caraway or cumin. It has a bitter and pungent taste and its flavour is similar to anise and oregano. This spice smells almost exactly like thyme but is more aromatic and less subtle in taste. Even a small amount of *Ajwain* tends to dominate the flavour of a dish.

Amchur (Dried green mango powder)

This is used for imparting a strong sour taste.

Asafoetida (*Hing*)

This is used in small quantities for imparting a strong smell. It is considered very healthy for digestive purposes though some people may find the smell unpleasant and strong. Don't use your saffron with *Hing*, therefore, ever!

Cardamom (*Elaichi*)

Please note that the left hand side picture is of brown cardamom and the right hand side picture is of green cardamom.

These come in two varieties: one is small, pale-green and the other is large and brown/black. The pale green variety is used in many Indian dishes including desserts. The brown variety is used for making curries or *pulaos*, but not in sweetmeats.

Chilli (Kashmiri Red variety)

In our recipes, we have suggested the use of Kashmiri Red Chillies as these impart a nice red colour and are not as hot as are the other red chillies. In case, you like your food to be really hot, then you can use the other red chillies available in the market which are much hotter.

Cinnamon (*Dalchini*)

This looks like the thin bark of a tree and imparts a lovely flavour both to the sweet and curried dishes. In India, however, it is more used for curries as Indians like Cardamom in their desserts much more than Cinnamon.

Cloves (*Laung*

These look like dried flower buds and add a lovely flavour to the food. Cloves are supposed to have antiseptic qualities which helps preserve food.

Coconut (*Nariyal)* powder or milk

This is used commonly in many South Indian and coastal Indian preparations.

Coriander seeds and fresh green leaves (*Dhania* and *Dhania patta*)

The dried seeds of Coriander form an essential part of Indian curries and are used quite extensively. The fresh green leaves are used for making Chutneys (Indian sauce) as well as for sprinkling on curries. Since the fresh leaves have a strong flavour, they should only be used by those who really like the flavour.

Cumin seeds (*Jeera*)

Cumin is another essential ingredient of Indian cuisine and is generally the first spice to go into the heated cooking oil before other items are added.

Curry leaves (*Kare-patta*)

These leaves have a lovely flavour and are absolutely essential if you like South Indian cuisine. In India, it grows in abundance and so is easily the cheapest herb to use. Generally used fresh, these can also be dried and used as they retain much of their fragrance even in the dried form.

Fennel (*Saunf*)

This is used for making some dishes and forms a part of the *Pach Phoran* (which shall be discussed later).

Fenugreek (*Methi*)

These are small flat seeds which have a slightly bitter flavour and must be used only in the quantities prescribed. They add quite a piquant flavour to the curries or dry dishes they are added to which are liked by many Indians. Lately, Fenugreek has acquired quite a cult status because of its almost magical effect in reducing the severity of Diabetes.

Garam Masala

This is a mixture in equal quantities of cinnamon, cloves, cardamom (both pale-green and brown variety) and whole black pepper corns. These can be ground together and kept in air tight containers for future use for up to a week. Some dishes can also be made by putting the whole spices in oil/ clarified butter (*Ghee*).

All lovers of Indian cooking must learn to use this mixture properly. If you cook Indian dishes only occasionally, you may be tempted to use the commercially available *Garam Masala* powders. Please remember, however, that to economize on costs, some manufacturers skimp on the more expensive ingredients mentioned above and instead add lots of coriander powder, cumin powder, turmeric powder, red chilli powder etc. to add volume. They even add *Kastoori Methi* which just drowns the subtle flavours of other *Garam Masalas*. So do check before you buy such a ready mix of spices.

Mustard seeds black (*Rai*)

These are black mustard seeds which look the same as the yellow variety but are supposed to be more pungent than their yellow cousins. This mustard seed is used a lot in South Indian and Western Indian cooking.

Onion seeds dried (*Mangrela* or *Kalonji*)

This spice is generally used as a part of the *Pach Phoran* (which is discussed below).

Pachphoran

Literally, a mixture of five spices namely black mustard seeds, cumin seeds, fenugreek seeds, fennel seeds and dried onion seeds, mixed in equal proportion, this category is regularly used in quite a few Eastern Indian dishes.

Turmeric (*Haldi*)

This is easily the commonest and the most important ingredient in any Indian curry dish. Though it does not have much of a flavour, it has a dark yellow colour and a lot of therapeutic value.

Yoghurt (*Dahi*)

Not really a spice or herb, yoghurt is frequently used in many Indian dishes. The variety used in cooking is cultured yoghurt and is always unflavoured. That way it comes closest to the Greek variety of yoghurt.

Please note that if you buy ready-made yoghurt from the supermarket, sometimes it splinters when you heat it. This presents an ungainly sight when you are, for example, cooking fish with yoghurt.

If you so desire then, you can very easily make yoghurt at home using the following method:

First, to start the whole process, you will need to buy some yoghurt. Subsequently about two tablespoons from the yoghurt you make can suffice to make the next home-made batch of yoghurt.

Ingredients

Milk-1 litre (4 cups)

Plain Unsweetened Yoghurt (as starter)-2 tablespoon

Method

Boil the milk well.

Tip: If you don't boil well, your yoghurt will set but will be a little sticky as factory-made yoghurts generally are.

Let the milk cool down to a level where it feels warm but not hot.

You should be able to use your finger for touching the milk without any fear of scalding it.

Beat the yoghurt well and gently add the warm milk.

Mix well.

Now pour this mixture into a bowl and place it in an insulated casserole.

I use an insulated lunch box which has a small heating element built-in. I need to "switch on" this lunch-box for about 30 minutes in really cold weather (where indoor temperatures be below 15 degree C or 59 degree F)

The basic idea is that the milk should remain warm for at least the next three hours.

After that the yoghurt sets on its own.

It is generally advisable to set the yoghurt at night so that you can have fresh yoghurt in the morning.

This also ensures that the vessel is not moved during the entire period that the yoghurt is setting because movement spoils the setting.

Prep Time: 5 minutes

Setting Time: 5 hours (minimum three hours)

A Big Thank You for Reading This Book till the End

Thank you so much for purchasing my book.

I know that you could have picked up other similar books on this subject matter but you took a chance with my book.

So a big THANKS for purchasing this book and reading it all the way to the end. If you liked this book, I shall be grateful if you could do me a small favour. Please take a moment to leave a review on Amazon, if you are happy.

If not, please tell me directly. Your feedback is of immense value to me as an Author. Your suggestions will help me in writing the kind of books that you love.

Your FREE Gift

As a way of saying thanks for your purchase, I'm offering FREE (worth $3.99 on all major e-book retailers) my Amazon #1 best-seller "**The Ultimate Guide to Cooking Rice the Indian Way**".

This is a LIMITED TIME OFFER.

From a Bed for Curries, to Pilaf, Biryani, Khichdi, Idli, Dosa, Savouries and Desserts, No One Cooks Rice as Lovingly as the Indians Do...

To get a FREE copy of this best-selling cookbook, please click here:

https://authormarketing.booklaunch.io/prasenjeetk umar@hotmail.com/ultimateguidetorice

Other Books By The Author

HOME STYLE INDIAN COOKING IN A JIFFY

Amazon #1 Best Seller in Indian and Professional Cooking

With an amazing compilation of over 100 delectable Indian dishes, many of which you can't get in any Indian restaurant for love or for money, this is unlike any other Indian Cook book. What this book focuses on is what Indians eat every day in their homes.

 To know more, do please go to:

https://authormarketing.booklaunch.io/prasenjeetk umar@hotmail.com/home-style-indian-cooking-in-a-jiffy

HOW TO COOK IN A JIFFY EVEN IF YOU HAVE NEVER BOILED AN EGG BEFORE

Amazon Top 5 Best Seller in Cooking for One

Never boiled an egg before but want to learn the magic art of cooking? Then don't leave home without this Survival Cookbook.

To know more, do please go to:

https://authormarketing.booklaunch.io/prasenjeetk umar@hotmail.com/how-to-cook-in-a-jiffy

HEALTHY COOKING IN A JIFFY: THE COMPLETE NO FAD NO DIET HANDBOOK

Amazon #1 in Hot New Releases in Health, Fitness & Dieting> Special Diets> Healthy

Amazon #3 Best Seller in Health, Fitness & Dieting> Special Diets> Healthy

If you are sick of dieting, counting calories, or gorging on supplements, do consider investing in this book of simply sensible cooking and get on to a journey of eternal joy and happiness.

To know more, do please go to:

https://authormarketing.booklaunch.io/prasenjeetk umar@hotmail.com/healthy-cooking-in-a-jiffy

THE ULTIMATE GUIDE TO COOKING LENTILS THE INDIAN WAY

Amazon #1 Best Seller in Indian Cooking and Rice & Grains

Presenting 58 Tastiest Ways to Cook Lentils as Soups, Curries, Snacks, Full Meals and hold your breath, Desserts! As only Indians can.

To know more, do please go to:

https://authormarketing.booklaunch.io/prasenjeetkumar@hotmail.com/lentils-cookbook

Books by the Author in the Quiet Phoenix Series

CELEBRATING QUIET PEOPLE: UPLIFTING STORIES FOR INTROVERTS AND HIGHLY SENSITIVE PERSONS

** This book is PERMA-FREE on all major online e-book retailers. If you are interested in this self-help genre for introverts or in the Quiet Phoenix series, it may be a good idea to sample my work through this book first. If you wish, you may also download this book from my blog.

Here is the link:

https://authormarketing.booklaunch.io/prasenjeetkumar@hotmail.com/celebrating-quiet-people**

A unique collection of motivational, inspirational and uplifting TRUE stories for introverts and highly sensitive persons that you shouldn't miss....

QUIET PHOENIX: AN INTROVERT'S GUIDE TO RISING IN CAREER & LIFE

Amazon #1 Best Seller in Legal Profession and Ethics & Professional Responsibility

Like the legendary Phoenix bird rising from the ashes, "Quiet Phoenix" is an incredible story that Prasenjeet Kumar shares, with wit and charm, of the journey from being a Corporate Lawyer to becoming a Full Time Author-Entrepreneur using his introversion as a strength to overcome all obstacles.

To know more, do please go to:

https://authormarketing.booklaunch.io/prasenjeetk umar@hotmail.com/quietphoenix

QUIET PHOENIX 2: FROM FAILURE TO FULFILMENT: A MEMOIR OF AN INTROVERTED CHILD

Amazon #1 Hot New Releases in Biographies & Memoirs > Professional and Academics > Educators

Celebrating The Quiet Child: A Must Read For every Parent, Teacher, Mentor, Sports Coach........

The underlying theme of the book is that just as a Phoenix Bird is hardwired to be reborn from the ashes of her ancestors, her tears are meant to cure wounds and she symbolises undying hope and optimism, so is your Quiet child built for persistence, creativity, and self-discipline; and for displaying a knack for self-learning, high emotional intelligence and an impeccable sense of moral responsibility.

To know more, do please go to:

https://authormarketing.booklaunch.io/prasenjeetkumar@hotmail.com/quietphoenix2-priced

Books by the Author in the Self-Publishing Without Spending a Dime Series

HOW TO BE AN AUTHOR ENTREPRENEUR WITHOUT SPENDING A DIME

** This book is PERMA-FREE on all major online e-book retailers. If you are interested in writing and self-publishing, you may want to download this book for FREE from my blog.

Here is the link:

https://authormarketing.booklaunch.io/prasenjeetkumar@hotmail.com/how-to-be-an-author-entrepreneur-without-spending-a-dime

This FREE e-book contains everything you need to know about self-publishing and also contains a list of helpful video tutorials and resources.

HOW TO TRANSLATE YOUR BOOKS WITHOUT
SPENDING A DIME

Enca$h the power of translation WITHOUT
SPENDING A DIME

To learn more, do please go to:

https://booklaunch.io/prasenjeetkumar@hotmail.c
om/how-to-translate-priced

Connect With The Author

Feel free to write to me anytime at ciaj@cookinginajiffy.com.

I would also love to connect with you on Social Media. Join me on:

Facebook:

https://www.facebook.com/cookinginajiffy

Twitter:

https://twitter.com/CookinginaJiffy

Goodreads:

https://www.goodreads.com/prasenjeet

Google Plus:

https://www.google.com/+PrasenjeetKumarAuthor

About The Author

Prasenjeet Kumar is a Law graduate from the University College London (2005-2008), London University and a Philosophy Honours graduate from St. Stephen's College (2002-2005), Delhi University. In addition, he holds a Legal Practice Course (LPC) Diploma from College of Law, Bloomsbury, London.

Prasenjeet loves gourmet food, music, films, golf and travelling. He has already covered seventeen countries including Canada, China, Denmark, Dubai, Germany, Hong Kong, Indonesia, Macau, Malaysia, Sharjah, Sweden, Switzerland, Thailand, Turkey, UK, Uzbekistan, and the USA.

Prasenjeet is the self-taught designer, writer, editor and proud owner of the website cookinginajiffy.com which he has dedicated to his mother. He is also running another website publishwithprasen.com where he shares tips about writing and self-publishing.

Index

www.ingramcontent.com/pod-product-compliance
Lightning Source LLC
Chambersburg PA
CBHW050918220726
PP18604600001B/15